# SO TO SPEAK 2

# SO TO SPEAK 2

## Integrating Speaking, Listening, and Pronunciation

**Megan Webster**

**Judy DeFilippo**
Northeastern University

Houghton Mifflin Company    Boston   New York

Director of ESL Programs: Susan Maguire
Senior Associate Editor: Kathleen Sands Boehmer
Editorial Associate: Kevin M. Evans
Senior Project Editor: Kathryn Dinovo
Senior Manufacturing Coordinator: Sally Culler
Marketing Manager: Patricia Fossi

Cover design: Harold Burch Designs, NYC

Illustrations: Brian Orr

Photo credits: p. 78 (top left), Peter Menzel/Stock Boston; (top right), Jose L. Pelaez/ The Stock Market; (bottom left), A. & J. Verkaik/The Stock Market; (bottom right), Ray Soto/The Stock Market; p. 91 (left), Daniel Brody/Stock Boston; (center), Lionel Delevingne/Stock Boston; (right), Sanford/Agliolo/The Stock Market.

Text credits: p. 69, exercise B: Adam Rogers and David A. Kaplan, "Get Ready for Nanotechnology," *Newsweek* Special Technology Issue, 1997, pp. 52–53; p. 88, L. Saxe, "Lying: Thoughts of an Applied Social Psychologist," *American Psychologist,* April 1991, pp. 409–415.

Printed in the U.S.A.

Library of Congress Catalog Card Number: 98-72015

ISBN: 0-395-87406-8

123456789-CS-03 02 01 00 99

*To all our students—the joy of our careers*

# CONTENTS

www.hmco.com/college

# SCOPE AND SEQUENCE

| UNIT AND TOPIC | LISTENING SKILLS | SPEAKING SKILLS | CORE LANGUAGE FOR PRODUCTION | PRONUNCIATION FEATURE |
|---|---|---|---|---|
| **UNIT 1** WHAT SHALL WE DO ON THE WEEKEND? | • Gist<br>• Specific information | • Expressing preferences<br>• Making plans<br>• Reporting<br>• Inviting and accepting<br>• Describing | • Simple present<br>• Present continuous<br>• Simple past<br>• *There is/are . . .*<br>• Adverbs of frequency<br>• *Would you like to go . . .*<br>• *Going to* (future reference) | /ʃ/ ship  /tʃ/ chip |
| **UNIT 2** DEALS ON WHEELS | • Specific information<br>• Details | • Describing people/emotional states<br>• Comparing<br>• Evaluating<br>• Giving opinions<br>• Asking for/giving information | • Simple present<br>• Present continuous<br>• *Can/can't*<br>• Comparative forms<br>• Descriptive adjectives | Syllable stress in adjectives of two or more syllables |
| **UNIT 3** WHAT ARE YOU LIKE? | • Specific information<br>• Prediction | • Describing physical/character traits/things<br>• Comparing<br>• Giving opinions | • Simple present<br>• Descriptive adjectives<br>• Comparative forms<br>• *I would not like a . . .*<br>• *To be*<br>• *She should . . . because . . .* | Syllable stress in adjectives with prefixes |
| **UNIT 4** TALK ABOUT YOUR COUNTRY | • Main ideas<br>• Details | • Describing countries/topography/attitudes<br>• Guessing | • Simple present<br>• *There is/are . . .*<br>• *Has/have*<br>• *Can/can't*<br>• Present perfect | Syllable stress in multisyllable nouns |

| UNIT AND TOPIC | LISTENING SKILLS | SPEAKING SKILLS | CORE LANGUAGE FOR PRODUCTION | PRONUNCIATION FEATURE |
|---|---|---|---|---|
| **UNIT 5** GET THE MESSAGE! | • Specific information<br>• Prediction<br>• Inference | • Leaving/ completing/ answering messages<br>• Giving opinions<br>• Reporting<br>• Predicting | • Simple present<br>• Simple past<br>• *Can/can't*<br>• Present continuous | /a/ not  /**ow**/ note<br>/**aw**/ out |
| **UNIT 6** KEEPING FIT | • Gist<br>• Attitude | • Describing<br>• Evaluating<br>• Comparing<br>• Giving opinions | • Simple present<br>• *Has/have*<br>• Comparatives/ superlatives<br>• *I think the pros are . . .*<br>• *You need to . . .*<br>• Simple future | Sentence stress |
| **UNIT 7** WHAT ARE YOU AFRAID OF? | • Specific information<br>• Prediction | • Identifying<br>• Predicting<br>• Describing<br>• Expressing feelings of fear<br>• Making suggestions | • Simple present<br>• Simple past<br>• *Petrified/terrified of . . .*<br>• *Can/can't*<br>• *I try to/try not to . . .* | Focus words |
| **UNIT 8** WATCH OUT! | • Gist<br>• Inference | • Describing road incident/ feelings<br>• Predicting<br>• Inferring<br>• Analyzing<br>• Narrating | • Simple present<br>• Present continuous<br>• Adjectives<br>• *Wh-* questions<br>• Simple past | /ɪ/ hit  /**iy**/ heat |
| **UNIT 9** WHAT ARE YOUR PLANS? | • Main ideas and details | • Describing<br>• Predicting<br>• Interviewing<br>• Agreeing/ disagreeing<br>• Giving opinions | • Simple present<br>• Simple future<br>• *Wh-* questions<br>• Gerund as subject<br>• Future continuous | Selected reductions |
| **UNIT 10** IN THE FUTURE | • Main ideas<br>• Details | • Predicting<br>• Guessing<br>• Describing<br>• Giving opinions<br>• Showing advantages | • Simple present<br>• Simple future<br>• Present continuous<br>• Present perfect<br>• *It would improve . . .*<br>• *Can/can't* | /l/  and  /r/ |

| UNIT AND TOPIC | LISTENING SKILLS | SPEAKING SKILLS | CORE LANGUAGE FOR PRODUCTION | PRONUNCIATION FEATURE |
|---|---|---|---|---|
| **UNIT 11**<br>HAVE YOU HEARD THE NEWS? | • Summary of main ideas<br>• Details | • Giving news<br>• Predicting<br>• Describing<br>• Reporting<br>• Summarizing<br>• Identifying feelings<br>• Interviewing | • Simple present<br>• Adjectives<br>• Simple past<br>• Present continuous<br>• Adjectives<br>• Past passive<br>• Adverbs of frequency | Focus words expansion |
| **UNIT 12**<br>ARE YOU TELLING THE TRUTH | • Summary of main ideas<br>• Prediction | • Advising<br>• Describing<br>• Analyzing<br>• Summarizing<br>• Identifying feelings<br>• Giving opinions<br>• Predicting<br>• Interviewing | • Simple present<br>• Present continuous<br>• Simple past<br>• *She should tell . . .*<br>• *It's interesting that . . .* | Rhythm |
| **UNIT 13**<br>ENVIRON-MENTALIST OF THE YEAR | • Main ideas | • Describing<br>• Evaluating<br>• Explaining<br>• Questioning<br>• Interviewing<br>• Giving opinions | • Simple present<br>• Simple past<br>• *Can/can't*<br>• Tag questions<br>• *I think it's important to . . .*<br>• *Should get/have* | Intonation |
| **UNIT 14**<br>STARTING YOUR OWN BUSINESS | • Main ideas<br>• Details | • Describing<br>• Evaluating<br>• Giving opinions<br>• Predicting<br>• Comparing | • Simple present<br>• *There is/are . . .*<br>• Comparative forms<br>• Superlative forms<br>• *It's important to . . .*<br>• Simple future<br>• *Going to* (future reference) | /f/ /v/ /b/ /p/ in initial position |
| **UNIT 15**<br>GIVE YOUR OPINION | • Opinions | • Asking for/giving opinions<br>• Agreeing/ disagreeing<br>• Reporting<br>• Interviewing<br>• Narrating | • Simple present<br>• Simple past<br>• Comparative/ superlative forms<br>• *It is important to . . .* | /t/ /θ/ think /s/ |

# TO THE TEACHER

*So to Speak* is an integrated speaking, listening, and pronunciation series for high-beginning and low intermediate students of English as a second or foreign language. Each book consists of fifteen self-contained units with high-interest but familiar and accessible topics for learners of English. The series is primarily designed for use in community colleges, pre-university programs, proprietary schools, and adult education.

The main goal of the series is fluency. With the aid of stimulating, theme-related activities, learners move smoothly through cohesive units, from topic warm-up tasks to relevant expressions, vocabulary, pronunciation, listening, speaking, and outside class follow-up assignments. Each section builds upon the preceding one to provide integrated practice in the oral skills.

Teachers may select units according to class needs and interests, but because units are structurally and lexically graded to a large extent, using them in order is recommended. This way, students have the benefit of recycled language, pronunciation features, as well as the Review and Taking Stock sections. The core language listed for each unit in the Scope and Sequence chart does not restrict the student with more language knowledge. It simply indicates the minimum language requirement to accomplish the speaking tasks.

## FEATURES

*So to Speak* is an entirely student-centered text with a clear format and easy-to-follow instructions. Here are some general guidelines about organizing the classroom to facilitate the use of this text:

- Make sure the seating is suitable for pair and group work when needed.
- Encourage students to use the *Express!* questions to speed up their learning.
- Maintain an encouraging environment and supervise unobtrusively.
- Hope for accuracy but be prepared to accept approximation.
- Accept developmental errors.
- Use native speaker strategies when language errors cause a breakdown in communication: *You mean Yuko is saying that...*
- Resist the temptation to interrupt fluency activities to correct language or pronunciation "mistakes." Instead, make a note of points that need attention and review them in a separate lesson.
- Keep in mind that the goal in the "Pronunciation Focus" section is awareness-raising.

## THE SERIES

*So to Speak* features two student books. Book 1 is geared toward high-beginning ESL students, whereas Book 2 is more appropriate for low-intermediate students. An audio cassette program accompanies each book. It includes all "Pronunciation Focus" and "Listening Focus" activities. We recommend that the books be used as a series, as some pronunciation features in Book 1 are not repeated in Book 2, and some features in the latter build on those presented in Book 1.

## UNIT ORGANIZATION

### Introduction

This section consists of an opening illustration or photograph with tasks to stimulate students' interest in the topic. Warm-up tasks vary, but they usually contain some topic-related language presented naturally. Sometimes, students are asked to describe people or events in the picture and expand on the topic in pair activities, and then share their ideas with the class.

### Language Focus

This section focuses on the vocabulary, idioms, and other expressions that students need to comprehend the listening text and participate in the speaking activities. Students participate in an array of challenging exercises that encourage maximum student involvement.

### Pronunciation Focus

The goal of this section is awareness-raising through exercises that focus on sound recognition, manipulation, discrimination, and controlled contextual practice. A systematic coverage of all pronunciation features is not the intention. Rather, high-frequency segmentals and suprasegmentals that cause trouble for beginning learners are presented with topic contexts in which they are likely to arise naturally. Particular attention is given to stress because of its unique importance in intelligibility. Communicative practice of pronunciation elements occurs naturally in the fluency sections that follow.

### Listening Focus

In this section, the main topic of the unit is presented in a variety of forms: for example, short informal conversations, TV and radio interviews, and simple mini lectures. Different, challenging, and fun, listening activities then allow students to practice skills such as prediction, gist, main ideas, details, specific information, inference, attitude, and feelings.

### Speaking Focus

This section involves a wide range of activities with problem-solving and information gap elements: discussions, role plays, socio-dramas, surveys, quizzes, games, and contests. Included here is the "Cross-Cultural Connection" feature in which students share their different cultural perspectives on a topic or issue. Performed in pairs or small groups, many of the activities ultimately lead to sharing ideas or results with the class—in other words, a cooperative learning approach. This approach, along with the accessible nature of the tasks produces a nonthreatening climate that fosters natural communication in the target language.

### Follow Up

This section has suggestions for assignments to be done outside the classroom and later reported to the group. Students may be asked to obtain information from an agency, flyer, or newspaper, make a telephone call, conduct a simple interview or survey, prepare a short talk, or do a word puzzle.

## UNIT GUIDELINES

### Introduction

The time needed for this section will vary according to the language level of the class and the time that can be allowed for any spontaneous discussion that arises from questions. Because fluency is a concern in this section, time flexibility is encouraged.

Most of the language required for the unit's activities is clearly presented, and appropriate for low-intermediate learners. A glance at the Core Language for Production listed in the "Scope and Sequence" chart shows whether you need to introduce a new structure or review a language item before embarking on a unit.

### Language Focus

The *Express!* feature is located in this section. Give students an opportunity to practice this tactic as it will help them navigate lessons, and therefore speed up their learning. The vocabulary and expressions in this section are crucial for the listening and speaking tasks that follow, so allow enough time to cover them adequately.

### Pronunciation Focus

The simple instructions to produce sounds should be helpful, but they are not expected to bring perfect results. Remember that awareness-raising is the main goal of this section. However, some students may ask for more practice with a particular pronunciation feature that causes them trouble. Encourage them to relax and enjoy the last practice segment: to read, or recite as the case may be, with expression and rhythm. These short conversations, limericks, or verse-like lines are especially designed to accentuate the stress and rhythm of English.

### Listening Focus

Depending on the proficiency level of your students, you may need to play the tape more times than specified in the book. The instructions for checking answers in the listening activities are designed to be nonthreatening and helpful, especially for those students who may have trouble with listening. With cooperative class effort, everyone should arrive at the correct answers.

### Speaking Focus

To maintain focus on the tasks, you might want to discuss the amount of time needed for each segment of pair or group work with the students beforehand. This is the longest part of the lesson, and the part where students have most freedom to experiment with language and develop fluency. Therefore, this is where most of the extra time should be allotted to avoid rushing to finish activities.

### Follow Up

Instructions should be clarified for assignments to be completed outside of class. Tell students how they will be expected to share the assignments in the following class. Although the activities are designed to be done outside of class, those that do not require any kind of research or group involvement could obviously be done in class if desired. If the material presented in this section is insufficient for the length of your course, you might consider adding guidelines for prepared talks, task-based trips, interactive information-seeking assignments, or active listening tasks.

### Review

As well as providing additional practice, this section will give you an idea of how students are progressing.

### Taking Stock

Encourage students to follow the suggestions for improvement and to report at mutually agreed intervals to the class and teacher about their accomplishments. EFL teachers will need to adapt some of the suggestions to the English speaking resources available in their country.

### Additional Guidelines

More material, including teacher notes, is available on our Web site.

## ACKNOWLEDGMENTS

First, we wish to thank our students, who have been the main source of inspiration for this series.

We would like to recognize the following outstanding colleagues with whom we have exchanged ideas over many years of teaching and writing: Charlotte Hester, Jay Ryan, Barbara Swartz, Janet Gottlieb, Susan Donio, and Eleanor Lander, Northeastern University, Boston; Pamela Graham, Boston University; and Libby Williams. We wish to give special thanks to Cathy Sadow and Linda Gajdusek of Northeastern University for their support.

Also, we would like to express our gratitude to the reviewers for their invaluable comments and suggestions during the development of the text: Silvia Gonzalez, LaGuardia Community College; Jaime Herbertsen, ELS Language Center, St. Petersburg, FL; Laura LaFlair, Northern Virginia Community College; Patricia Pashby, University of San Francisco; Patricia Rice, Long Island University; Janine Rudnick, El Paso Community College; and Diane Ruggiero, Broward Community College.

We also wish to thank Joann Rishel Kozyrev for all her useful comments and suggestions, and give a special thanks to Kathy Sands Boehmer for her patience and editorial expertise, and Susan Maguire for her insightful guidance, nurturing, and support during each stage of the project.

Finally, a very special thanks to our families, whose love and encouragement sustained us throughout.

# TO THE STUDENT

*So to Speak* helps you understand native speakers of English and also teaches you how to communicate with them. You will listen to natural language, learn vocabulary and expressions that native speakers of English use every day, and learn how to pronounce English words properly.

Don't worry if you don't understand everything on the tape. Don't be afraid to speak. Don't worry if you make mistakes. Just listen and talk as much as you can. This is how your speaking, listening, and pronunciation skills will improve.

There are explanations in the units about when to use the *Express!* questions below. Practice these *Express!* questions and use them to help you learn fast.

For more practice after each unit, visit our Web site at http://www.hmco.com/college.

Relax and enjoy the course!

## Unit

**1**  What is a *CALENDAR?*
   What is an *ASSOCIATION?*
   What does *TEMPERATURE* mean?

**2**  I can't hear. Could you please speak louder?
   I can't hear the tape. Could you please turn it up?

**3**  Could you please speak slower?
   I didn't catch that. Could you please repeat it?

**4**  How do you spell . . . ? Could you please write it on the board?
   Could you please pronounce this word for me?

**5**  Sorry, but I don't understand what to do.
   Which page are we on?
   Can you please help me with this *EXERCISE?*

**6**  What is the answer to *NUMBER 5,* please?
   Which is the correct answer to that question?

**7**  What is the homework for today?
   Could you please explain the assignment to me?

**8**    What is the word for that? (Point to it.)
What do you call *SIGNS THAT SAY THINGS LIKE "NO SMOKING"?*
How do you spell it?

**9**    It's very hot. May I open the window?
It's very cold. Would you mind if I closed the window?
There is a lot of noise outside, and I can't hear. May I close the window?

**10**    What is the difference between *BROUGHT UP* and *BROUGHT ABOUT?*
Could you please show me how to use them in sentences?

**11**    Excuse me for interrupting, but I don't understand the *QUESTION/ANSWER.*
Would you please explain it again?

**12**    Can I talk to you for a moment after class about the *ASSIGNMENT?*
I have something to ask you.
Can I make an appointment to see you? I need to talk to you about . . .

**13**    I'll erase the board for you.
Can I help you hand out the *PAPERS?*
I'll carry *THE BOOKS* for you.

**14**    Sorry I'm late. *I OVERSLEPT.*
*I FORGOT TO SET THE ALARM.*
*THE TRAFFIC WAS BAD.*
*I MISSED THE BUS.*

**15**    May I please leave class early today? *I HAVE TO GO TO THE DOCTOR.*
*I HAVE TO MEET MY SISTER AT THE AIRPORT.*

# 1 What Shall We Do on the Weekend?

## INTRODUCTION

**A** Talk about the pictures and what the people are doing.

EXAMPLE *There are a lot of people in a stadium watching a ...*

**B** **PAIR WORK.** Read the calendar listing. Find the listing for each event in the pictures. Take turns and tell the class all the details about the event in one picture. Include this information:

- what the event is and where it is
- on which day and at what time it takes place
- how much it costs
- if it's cheap or expensive

**Movies (cont.)**
**Cinema 6,** Mission Creek.
*Killer on the Loose.* 1:30, 3:00, 7:00, 9:00
*Love in the Mall.* 2:30, 4:30, 6:30, 8:30
**Odeon**, Main Plaza.
*Horror in Space.* 2:15, 5:00, 8:45
*Reach for the Moon.* 11:30, 2:30, 5:30, 9:00

**Museums (cont.)**
**Maritime Museum**. 17th century ships. 10–4. $3.
**Modern Art**. Chinese Art. Jan. to June. Daily 10 to 6. Admission $8. Students $5.
**American Heritage**. Sculptures. American West. 10 to 5 p.m. Closed Mon. Free Sat. 12 to 5.
**Satch Gallery**. Fashion Photography. 11–4. $5.

**Outdoors**
**Grand Stadium.** Football. Sat. 2 p.m. $25, $10.
**Shore Parachutes.** Skydiving instruction. 2 hour sessions. 8 a.m. to 8 p.m. 856-2176.
**Run/Skate/Bike Association.** Washington Park. Sun. 8 a.m. Free.
**Beach Volleyball Club.** Join us at Cray Beach! Sat. 8–5. Free.

**Music Scene**
**Chamber Music.** Olive Hall. Sat. 3 p.m. Bach, Mozart, Debussy. $15. Students & Seniors $10.
**Poppin' Chicks.** Grove Park. Sun. 4 p.m. Free.
**Charlton Annual Fest.** Music, international food and other attractions. Sun. 10 to 7. Free.
**Advent Church Choir.** American musical hits! Sat. 6:30 p.m. Admission $5. Children $2.

**C** Tell the class about some events in the calendar that interest you. Explain why.

EXAMPLE *One event that interests me is ... because I like ... Another event ...*

# LANGUAGE FOCUS   *Topic-related expressions*

**Express!**

Practice these *Express!* questions to find the meanings of words:

*What is a CALENDAR?*

*What is an ASSOCIATION?*

*What does TEMPERATURE mean?*

**A** **PAIR WORK.** In "Listening Focus," you will hear these expressions. Find their meanings in the list below and write them on the correct lines. Check your answers with the class.

EXAMPLE   *"How about you, Sheila?" means . . .*

1. How about you, Sheila?   _____

2. What do you have in mind?   _____

3. Catch a show or movie   _____

4. Do our own thing   _____

5. Sounds good to me!   _____

6. They've got to be kidding!   _____

7. Bundle up   _____

8. Rain showers   _____

| | |
|---|---|
| It's a good idea! | Wear a lot of warm clothes |
| Rain off and on | What ideas do you have? |
| I don't believe them! | Go to a show or movie |
| What's Sheila going to do? | Do what we're interested in by ourselves |

**B** **PAIR WORK.** Complete the conversation with the above expressions, or a form of the expressions. Then role-play the conversation.

Chuck:   Are you doing anything tonight?

Sharon:  No. What _____ mind?

Chuck:   I'd like to _____ a movie after work.

Sharon:  _____ to me!

Chuck:   _____ Carl? Shall we ask him to go with us?

Sharon:  No, he likes to _____ his _____ thing.

Chuck:   We'd better _____ tonight.

Sharon:  Why? Is it going to be cold?

Chuck:   The temperature's dropping to 40°, and there'll be rain

_____.

Sharon:  You've _____!

**C** These expressions are in "Listening Focus" too. Take turns and use them to describe the recent weather in your city or state.

sunny     cloudy     winds     rain     cold     snow     temperature

EXAMPLE   *It was cold last week, but it didn't snow. Today it's . . .*

# PRONUNCIATION FOCUS /ʃ/ ship /tʃ/ chip

When you make the **sh** sound, your tongue touches your top teeth at the back. Look at the picture. In English, we make this sound when we want people to be quiet. Practice the **soft sh** sound:

ssshhh    ssshhh    ssshhh

When you make the **ch** sound, your tongue touches the part above your top front teeth as you blow. To help you make the **hard ch** sound, pretend you are an old steam engine!

choo-choo    choo-choo    choo-choo

**A** FIRST LISTENING

- Listen carefully to the words with **sh** and **ch** sounds.
- Listen again and repeat.

| | | | |
|---|---|---|---|
| sheep | cash | washing | admission |
| cheap | catch | watching | kitchen |

**B** SECOND LISTENING

- Listen to the sentences.
- Listen again and circle the word you hear in each sentence.
- Take turns reading a sentence to check your answers with the class.

1. Can you *cash / catch* this?
2. I want the *blue ship / chip*.
3. He wants his *share / chair*.
4. Yes, they are *sheep / cheap*.
5. She's *washing / watching* the baby.
6. The museum is on *Sash / Satch* Street.

**C** THIRD LISTENING: **GROUP WORK**

- Read these tongue twisters* aloud by yourself. Then listen to them.
- Practice reading the tongue twisters to your group.

Sherry sells cheap T-shirts on the shore each day the sun shines and makes a lot of cash, while Charlie plays chess on Mission Beach or goes fishing and eats fish and chips.

Butch works in a shoe shop chain on Sash Street called Choice Shoes, while his boss Chen sits in his kitchen chair munching on chow mein!

*Tongue twisters are groups of words that are difficult to say quickly.

**A** Read the information below about Rich, Charlie, and Sheila. Listen to them talking about their weekend plans. Rich starts the conversation. Circle the correct answers about their plans as you listen.

| | |
|---|---|
| Charlie is going to | a. play in the tennis championships. |
| | b. watch the tennis championships. |
| Rich is going to | a. go fishing at Shoal Bay. |
| | b. go surfing at Shoal Bay. |
| Sheila is going to | a. watch beach volleyball. |
| | b. play beach volleyball. |
| They are all going to | a. show a movie later. |
| | b. catch a movie later. |

They're all going to read the homework chapters on
    a. Saturday morning.
    b. Sunday morning.

On Sunday afternoon they are going to the park to
    a. listen to the Poppin' Chicks.
    b. listen to the Rockin' Ships.

**B** Listen again. Now check (✓) the weather forecast and write the temperatures in the chart as you listen.

| | | | | | | | |
|---|---|---|---|---|---|---|---|
| Friday | ☐ | ☐ | ☐ | ☐ | ☐ | ☐ | ☐ |
| Saturday | ☐ | ☐ | ☐ | ☐ | ☐ | ☐ | ☐ |
| Sunday | ☐ | ☐ | ☐ | ☐ | ☐ | ☐ | ☐ |

**C** Take turns reading a sentence to give a gist (general idea) of the weekend plans and the weather forecast.

EXAMPLE *Charlie is going to . . .    Rich is going to . . .    Friday is going to be . . . with a temperature of . . .*

**D** **PAIR WORK.** Rich, Charlie, and Sheila can't do what they planned because of the weather. Talk about what they can do instead. Tell the class.

EXAMPLE *They can go to . . . or . . .    They can stay home and . . .*

# SPEAKING FOCUS    *Making plans for the weekend*

**A** **GROUP WORK.** Which of these activities do you usually like to do on Saturday? Why? Check three activities. Talk about them with your group.

EXAMPLE    *I usually like to . . . and . . . on Saturday because . . .    What do you like to do on . . . ?*

___ go shopping          ___ go to the beach          ___ go dancing

___ watch TV             ___ have lunch out           ___ watch or play sports

___ listen to music      ___ hang out with friends    other: _____

**B** **GROUP WORK.** How about taking a tour on Sunday? Look at Dan's Cheap One-Day Tours. Plan your tour. Tell the other groups about it. Decide which group's tour is going to be the most interesting or the most fun.

EXAMPLE    *Tell us about your tour.*
*Well, we're going to . . .*
*That sounds interesting, but I think our plan is more . . .*

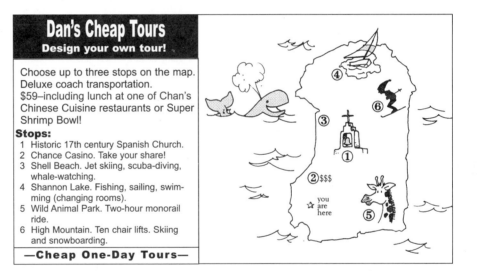

**Dan's Cheap Tours**
**Design your own tour!**

Choose up to three stops on the map. Deluxe coach transportation. $59–including lunch at one of Chan's Chinese Cuisine restaurants or Super Shrimp Bowl!

**Stops:**
1  Historic 17th century Spanish Church.
2  Chance Casino. Take your share!
3  Shell Beach. Jet skiing, scuba-diving, whale-watching.
4  Shannon Lake. Fishing, sailing, swimming (changing rooms).
5  Wild Animal Park. Two-hour monorail ride.
6  High Mountain. Ten chair lifts. Skiing and snowboarding.

**—Cheap One-Day Tours—**

*Cross-Cultural Connection*

**GROUP WORK.** Write down what young people and families do on a typical weekend in your hometown or country. Tell your group.

EXAMPLE    *Young people usually . . . on Saturday.*
*On Sunday . . .    Families often . . .*

Young People                          Families

_____                      _____

_____                      _____

_____                      _____

**A** Check the weekend weather forecast on TV and write it on the lines below.

**Saturday** _____

**Sunday** _____

Ask the class which TV channel they watched for the forecast. Is their forecast exactly the same as yours?

EXAMPLE *Which channel did you watch?   I watched Channel . . .*
*What's the forecast for Saturday?*

**B** Look for a newspaper with a calendar of events. Circle some things that interest you. Find a classmate to go with you to an event.

EXAMPLE *There's a science fiction movie playing at . . . that I'd like to see.*
*Is anyone interested in going with me?*
*There's a jazz fest at . . . on . . . The tickets are . . .*

**C** Read Chong's e-mail message to Stacy. Prepare a similar message to send to a friend or classmate about your weekend. Read it to your group.

```
To:      stacyb@acr.com
_____

Hi!
Shar and I went to the beach on Saturday. The sun
shone all day. But there was no shade, so I got
sunburned! But we had fun. Later, we went to a
really great show. We had heavy rain showers on
Sunday, so we just stayed home and watched TV.
How was your weekend?
```

**D** These words are in the calendar on page 1. Some read clockwise (⤷), others read counterclockwise (⤶). Find the words and write them on the lines. Then tell the class what they are.

EXAMPLE *The word in the first square is . . .   The word in the first triangle is . . .*

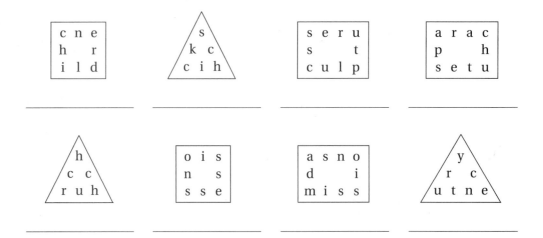

# 2 Deals on Wheels

## INTRODUCTION

**A** Look at the title and the picture. Describe the picture and what is happening.

> EXAMPLE   *The place is a . . .   There are . . . cars . . .   The woman is talking to the car salesman. I think she's . . .*

**B** Check (✓) the words that describe how the people look. Share your answers with the class.

| The customer looks | The salesman looks |
|---|---|
| ___ excited | ___ excited |
| ___ nervous | ___ nervous |
| ___ happy | ___ happy |
| ___ worried | ___ worried |
| ___ confident | ___ confident |

**C** **GROUP WORK.** Talk about the questions below.

> EXAMPLE   *A warranty is . . .   It's important to have a warranty because . . .*

1. There is a warranty in the picture. What is a warranty?

2. Why is it important to have one?

3. Which car do you think the woman will buy?

4. Which car do you like? Why?

# LANGUAGE FOCUS    *Parts of a car*

### Express!

Practice these *Express!* questions. When you can't hear, you say:

*I can't hear. Could you please speak louder? I can't hear the tape. Could you please turn it up?*

**A** **PAIR WORK.** Here are some parts of a car. Decide what the parts do. Write the name of each part on the line next to what it does. Check your answers with the class.

EXAMPLE    *The ignition key starts the car. The . . . warms the car.*

1. _ignition key_____ starts the car
2. _____ warms the car
3. _____ changes the car to another gear
4. _____ cools the car
5. _____ lets you stop or slow the car
6. _____ let you see when it's dark
7. _____ let you see when it rains
8. _____ accelerates the car

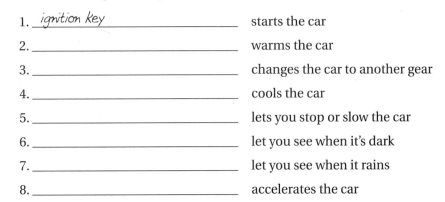

**B** Circle the meaning of each sentence. Then talk about your answers with the class.

EXAMPLE    *"It's in perfect condition" means . . .*

1. It's in perfect condition.
    a. It needs many repairs.
    b. It doesn't need repairs.

2. It's an automatic.
    a. It has a stick shift.
    b. It doesn't have a stick shift.

3. It's a classy car.
    a. The car is stylish.
    b. The car is ugly.

4. Take it out for a test drive.
    a. Drive the car on a highway.
    b. Take a driver's test.

5. It's economical.
    a. It saves you time.
    b. It saves you money.

6. It's reliable.
    a. You can depend on it.
    b. It is easy to drive.

# PRONUNCIATION FOCUS    *Stress in adjectives of two or more syllables*

Some words have one **syllable** or **sound part.** Other words have two or more syllables. When there are two or more syllables, one syllable is **long** and **strong.** In two-syllable adjectives, the stress is usually on the first syllable:

p<u>a</u>tient        ch<u>ea</u>per

In the adjectives below with three, four, or five syllables, the stress varies.

exp<u>e</u>nsive    d<u>a</u>ngerous    dep<u>e</u>ndable    econ<u>o</u>mical

 **A**    FIRST LISTENING

• Listen to these words. Listen again and repeat the words.

n<u>e</u>rvous      autom<u>a</u>tic      dep<u>e</u>ndable      w<u>o</u>rried      <u>i</u>nteresting

 **B**    SECOND LISTENING

• Read the following words aloud and guess which syllable is stressed. Underline the syllable.
• Listen to see if you underlined the right syllable in each word.
• Take turns saying the words with the correct stress to check your answers with the class.

| | | |
|---|---|---|
| 1. perfect | 5. beautiful | 9. excited |
| 2. expensive | 6. helpful | 10. classy |
| 3. economical | 7. special | 11. confident |
| 4. popular | 8. excellent | 12. reliable |

 **C**    THIRD LISTENING: **PAIR WORK**

• Read the conversation by yourself and underline the stressed syllables in the adjectives.
• Listen to check your answers.
• Choose your part. Listen again and repeat your lines.
• Role-play the conversation.

Mary:   Hey, Bob. Your new car is classy!

Bob:    Yeah, it's beautiful, isn't it!

Mary:   Yes. Was it expensive?

Bob:    Yes, but it's economical . . . thirty-five miles per gallon!

Mary:   And it's in excellent condition!

Bob:    Yeah, I'm very excited about it.

Mary:   Well, you really need a reliable car. You travel so much!

Bob:    I know. It's the perfect car for me!

**A** **1** Look at the chart before you listen to the conversation between a used car salesman and a customer. Listen and check (✓) the information that is correct about each car. The information about the Honda is started for you. Use an *Express!* question if you can't hear the tape.

| | | Honda | Ford | Mazda |
|---|---|---|---|---|
| **Condition:** | good | | | |
| | excellent | | | |
| | perfect | ✓ | | |
| **Price:** | $6,999 | | | |
| | $8,500 | ✓ | | |
| | $11,999 | | | |
| **Air Conditioning:** | yes | ✓ | | |
| | no | | | |
| **Shift:** | standard | | | |
| | automatic | | | |
| **Miles/Gallon:** | 25 | | | |
| | 28 | | | |
| | 30 | | | |

When you are finished, check your notes and talk about your answers with the class.

EXAMPLE    *The Honda's in . . . condition.*

**B** **PAIR WORK.** Read these questions. Listen again to the conversation and answer the questions. Share your answers with the class.

EXAMPLE    *She wants to buy the . . .    It costs . . .*

1. Which car does the woman really want to buy? Why?

2. Why doesn't she buy this car?

3. Why does she like the Mazda so much?

4. Is color important to her?

5. Is the salesman      a. patient      b. pushy      c. helpful      d. friendly? Explain.

# SPEAKING FOCUS    *Talking about cars*

**A** **GROUP WORK.** Check (✓) what you think are important things to consider when you buy a used car. Then tell your group. (Use an *Express!* question to find the meanings of words you don't know.)

EXAMPLE    *I think that . . . is very important when you buy a used car.*
           *I think . . . is more important than . . .*

| | | | |
|---|---|---|---|
| ___ size | ___ comfort | ___ price | ___ condition of motor |
| ___ style | ___ age | ___ color | ___ cost of repairs |
| ___ speed | ___ mileage | ___ dents | ___ air conditioning |
| ___ CD player | ___ size of engine | ___ miles per gallon | ___ other _____ |

**B** **GROUP WORK.** Talk about these cars and compare them. Include price, size, comfort, speed, and repair costs. Also, indicate which are the most popular and the most reliable.

EXAMPLE    *Well, the . . . is more expensive than the . . . but I think the most expensive is . . .*

| Van | Sedan | Sports Car | Station Wagon | Sport Utility Vehicle |

---

## Cross-Cultural Connection
### GROUP WORK.

1. Talk about the types of cars (sedans, vans, station wagons) that people drive in your native country or where you live now. Which are the most popular cars?

2. The woman is buying a car alone in the conversation you heard on the tape. Would a woman buy a car alone in your culture? Explain why or why not.

3. How do people usually buy a used car in your culture: from a car dealer, classified ads, or through friends? Explain.

4. In some U.S. states, people can drive at age sixteen. Is sixteen too young? At what age can you drive in other countries? Reach an agreement on a good age to get a driver's license and talk about it with the class.

   EXAMPLE    *We think a good age to get a driver's license is . . .*
              *I think that's too young. People should be . . .*

# FOLLOW UP

**A** Look at the ads for used cars in the "automotive" section of your local newspaper. Decide on a used car that you might like to buy. Before you call and ask for more information about this car, go back to section A of "Speaking Focus" in this unit to be sure you know all the vocabulary you will need.

Here are some sample questions to ask. Add two more questions you think are important.

1. What year is the car?

2. How many miles does it have?

3. How many miles per gallon does the car get?

4. Does the car have air conditioning? A CD player?

5. What color is it?

6. Does the car have any dents?

7. _____

8. _____

Now, telephone for more information about the car.

> EXAMPLE   *Hello. I'm calling about your car ad in the . . .   I have some questions. First, what year is the car?*

Share the information you learned with your classmates.

**B** Find out where electric or solar-powered cars are sold in your area, how much they cost, and why (or if) they are going to be "the cars of the future." Share the information with the class.

**C** Imagine that you have enough money to buy a new car, truck, or motorcycle. Which would you buy? What make or model would you buy? Why? Share your ideas with your group or class.

> EXAMPLE   *I would like to buy a . . .*

# 3  *What Are You Like?*

**A**  Look at the pictures. What do Liz and Dave look like? Describe them. Use these words to describe their physical appearance.

> EXAMPLE  *Liz is ... and ... with ... hair.*

| Height | Build | Hair |
|---|---|---|
| tall | thin, slim | short |
| average height | average build | long |
| short | heavy | straight or curly |

**B**  Describe and compare their rooms and desks. Use words from the list below and other words.

> EXAMPLE  *Liz's room is ...  It is ... than Dave's ...  Her desk ...*

> tidy (neat)      untidy (messy)      organized      disorganized

**C**  **PAIR WORK.** Read the conversation between Liz and Dave. Choose your parts and role-play the conversation. Then answer the questions.

> EXAMPLE  *Liz loaned Dave ...*

1. What did Liz loan Dave?

2. Why does she want it back?

3. Does Dave know where the article is?

4. Do you think he's going to take it to class?

5. Do you think he *really* found it useful?

# LANGUAGE FOCUS  *Descriptive adjectives*

**A** **PAIR WORK.** Talk about the meaning of the words in the list below. Use an *Express!* question if you need to. Complete the sentences with the correct word. Read a sentence each to check your answers with the class.

### Express!

Practice these *Express!* questions when you have trouble hearing or understanding:

*Could you please speak slower?*
*I didn't catch that.*
*Could you please repeat it?*

| sensible | patient | honest | caring | responsible |
|----------|---------|--------|--------|-------------|
| sensitive | reliable | generous | dependent | romantic |

1. Nora cares about her parents. She is a _____ person.

2. The teacher never gets mad with the students. He is very _____.

3. Katie depends on her husband to fix everything. She's a _____ person.

4. When Wes says he'll do something, he always does it. He's _____.

5. Ian is easily hurt by what people say. He is too _____.

6. Pamela never cheats. She is an _____ person.

7. Willy falls in love with every pretty girl he meets. He's so _____.

8. Ruth always gives her friends expensive presents. She's _____.

9. Ella studies hard and always does her homework. She's a _____ student.

10. Dave thinks carefully before making decisions. He is _____.

**B** **PAIR WORK.** Match each word below with its opposite. Check your answers with the class.

EXAMPLE   *The opposite of caring is uncaring.*

1. _e_ caring      a. dishonest
2. ___ patient      b. unromantic
3. ___ sensible      c. unreliable
4. ___ sensitive      d. ungenerous (stingy)
5. ___ dependent      e. uncaring
6. ___ responsible      f. insensitive
7. ___ reliable      g. impatient
8. ___ honest      h. independent
9. ___ romantic      i. irresponsible
10. ___ generous      j. impulsive

**C** **GROUP WORK.** Look at these words and their meanings. Use them to describe someone you know.

EXAMPLE   *My sister is bossy. She's always telling me what to do.*

| **neat** | tidy (a neat person) or nice (cool) |
|----------|-------------------------------------|
| **bossy** | always tells people what to do |
| **nosy** | wants to know everything about other people |

| | |
|---|---|
| **crabby** | always complains about something |
| **talkative** | talks all the time |
| **compassionate** | feels for people who are suffering |

## *PRONUNCIATION FOCUS*    *Syllable stress in adjectives with prefixes*

The first syllable is usually stressed in adjectives of two or three syllables. Prefixes are usually unstressed. The main stress remains on the same syllable.

EXAMPLE   *organized*   **dis***organized*   *passionate*   **com***passionate*

### A FIRST LISTENING

- Read aloud the words with these prefixes: **un, in, im, dis, ir.**
- Listen and repeat the words.

| | | | |
|---|---|---|---|
| unfriendly | unkind | uncaring | insensitive |
| impatient | dishonest | untidy | irresponsible |

### B SECOND LISTENING

- Read the paragraph. Guess what the missing **stressed** syllables are.
- Listen and write the **stressed** syllables in the spaces as you listen or in the pause at the end.
- Check your answers with the class by reading a sentence each.

Dale is a short, handsome man but very un_____ly. He is also im____tient, especially with the children. His dis____ganized wife, Joyce, is no better. She's ____kind to the children and sometimes is even dis____est with them. She screams at them and is in____sitive to their feelings. Dale and Joyce are irre_____sible parents. I think parents should be kind and com_____ionate with their children.

### C THIRD LISTENING: **PAIR WORK**

- Underline the stressed syllables in the adjectives.
- Choose your part. Then listen and repeat your lines.
- Role-play the conversation.

Ted:  What's your new boss like?

May:  Oh, he's kind of disorganized.

Ted:  I hope he's not impatient and insensitive like the last one!

May:  Not exactly. But he is kind of irresponsible.

Ted:  Oh, yeah. Then he's lucky to have a responsible, organized assistant like you.

May:  I guess so. But my colleagues say he's actually a caring, compassionate person.

**A**    **1** Read the list of words in the chart below. Yolanda is talking to Peggy on the phone. Listen to their conversation as Yolanda describes Larry, June, and Sam. Check (✓) the words on the chart that she uses to describe each of them.

| Description | Larry | June | Sam |
|---|---|---|---|
| tall | | | |
| average build | | | |
| straight hair | | | |
| short, curly hair | | | |
| insensitive | | | |
| sensible | | | |
| responsible | | | |
| impulsive | | | |
| unreliable | | | |
| disorganized | | | |
| unromantic | | | |
| romantic | | | |
| independent | | | |
| sensitive | | | |
| compassionate | | | |
| nervous | | | |
| impatient | | | |

**2** Take turns to expand the descriptions of Larry, June, and Sam.

> EXAMPLE    First student:    *Larry's ... and ...*
> Second student:  *He's also ...*

**B**    **PAIR WORK.** Listen again to the conversation and talk about these questions. Share your answers with the class.

> EXAMPLE    *Yolanda wants Peggy to meet Larry because ...*

1. Why does Yolanda want Peggy to meet Larry?

2. Why does Peggy want to know about Larry?

3. Why are Larry and June getting divorced?

# SPEAKING FOCUS  *Describing people (character qualities and physical appearance)*

**A** CLASS GAME! WHO IS IT?

How would you describe yourself? Make notes of your own description on a piece of paper and fold it.

EXAMPLES

*tall, heavy*  OR  *short, very beautiful!*

*long, straight black hair*     *long, curly hair*

*impulsive and nervous*     *independent, sensitive*

*but very intelligent!*     *disorganized but compassionate*

Form a circle. Pass your papers around until the teacher says, Stop! Describe the person on the paper you have. For example: *This student is tall, heavy, and . . . He or she is independent . . .* Students guess who it is. When they guess correctly, the student says, *Yes, it's me!*

**B** **GROUP WORK.** Write three things you would *not* like a teacher, a parent, and a politician to be. Talk about them with your group and give your reasons.

EXAMPLE  *First, I would not like a teacher to be . . . because . . .*

**Teacher**  _____  _____  _____

**Parent**  _____  _____  _____

**Politician**  _____  _____  _____

**C** **1 GROUP WORK.** Which man is right for Virginia? Decide who she should marry.

**VIRGINIA** (age 25)
tall, heavy build
policewoman
independent
sensible but bossy
likes motorbiking,
 rock music

**ERIC** (age 35)
tall and slim
businessman
talkative and nosy
impulsive, romantic
likes golf, dancing,
 rock music

**JOHN** (age 24)
short, average build
artist
patient, independent
sensitive, sensible, and
 reliable
likes hiking, romance movies

**2** Discuss your choice and the reasons for it with the other groups.

## Cross-Cultural Connection

**GROUP WORK.** Compare Americans with people in your native country or culture. Below are some words you can use.

EXAMPLE  *People in my country are more . . . than Americans.*

taller/shorter          more handsome/beautiful

more/less friendly      more patient/impatient

more/less romantic      more honest/dishonest

more/less nosy          more dependent/independent

**A** Read about the kind of woman Bobby would like to marry. Prepare to talk to your group or class about the kind of person you would like to marry. (If you are already married, talk about your husband or wife.)

> I would like to marry a beautiful, slim woman with long, curly hair. I would like her to be an independent, professional person and very organized. I am disorganized, and I would like her to teach me to be organized! I would also want her to be caring and compassionate.

**B** WORD PUZZLE

There are sixteen words from this unit in the puzzle. Words read from top to bottom, from bottom to top, from left to right, and from right to left. Find as many words as you can and circle them. Work with the class to put all the words on the board and take turns reading them.

| i | i | n | s | e | n | s | i | t | i | v | e |
|---|---|---|---|---|---|---|---|---|---|---|---|
| m | t | c | i | t | n | a | m | o | r | n | u |
| p | s | g | t | i | d | y | s | u | a | e | m |
| a | e | n | n | o | p | c | e | n | d | r | e |
| t | n | i | n | c | b | r | n | r | e | s | v |
| i | o | r | u | e | a | s | e | z | u | i |   |
| e | h | a | s | r | h | b | i | l | i | o | s |
| n | s | c | y | l | j | b | b | i | n | v | l |
| t | i | n | x | y | p | y | l | a | a | r | u |
| y | d | u | a | r | c | r | e | b | g | e | p |
| s | u | n | k | i | n | d | t | l | r | n | m |
| s | u | o | r | e | n | e | g | e | o | u | i |

**C** Think of someone you know very well. Prepare to talk about this person's physical appearance and character qualities. Describe the person to your group. Explain why you like or dislike this person.

> EXAMPLE  *I'm going to talk about . . .   He is . . .*

# 4  Talk about Your Country

## INTRODUCTION

Japan is an island country made up of four main islands and hundreds of smaller ones. More than 85 percent of Japan's land is covered with mountains. The oceans around Japan's chain of islands affect the climate. A warm ocean wind from the south allows people to swim almost all year round in tropical Okinawa. Polar winds from the north bring in colder temperatures to the island of Hokkaido, where people can ski on the snow-covered mountains.

**A**  Read the information about Japan. Underline the new words. If you can't figure out the meanings of these words, use an *Express!* question. Write the meanings on the lines. Then take turns saying a sentence to check your answers with the class.

EXAMPLE   *A chain of islands is . . .    Climate means . . .*

- chain of islands _____
- climate _____
- tropical _____
- polar _____
- snow-covered _____

**B**  **PAIR WORK.** Look at the map and talk about the following.

EXAMPLE   *Japan has . . . islands.*

- how many islands Japan has
- where you can go skiing
- where you can go swimming
- the countries that are near Japan

**Express!**

Practice these *Express!* questions. When you aren't sure how to spell or pronounce a word, you say:

*How do you spell . . . ? Could you please write it on the board? Could you please pronounce this word for me?*

**A**  **PAIR WORK.** Talk about the words below and their meanings. Complete the sentences that follow and check your answers. Then take turns reading the sentences to check your answers with the class. The first sentence has been completed for you.

| | |
|---|---|
| **export** | to send products outside a country to sell |
| **economy** | the financial condition of a country |
| **talent** | the ability to create and do beautiful work |
| **manufacture** | to produce or make |
| **craft** | a skill or ability in handwork or the arts |
| **pottery** | bowls, plates, and other items made from clay |
| **earthquake** | a movement of the earth under the ground |
| **weaver** | someone who makes cloth or fabric on a wooden machine called a loom |
| **unemployment** | a situation where people cannot find work |
| **honor** | respect and special attention |

1. The countries of Kuwait and Saudi Arabia ——*export*—— a lot of oil.

2. She makes beautiful cloth on a machine called a loom. She is a _____.

3. The Japanese government thinks its artists deserve special respect. It treats them with _____.

4. He makes bowls and vases from clay with his hands. His craft is _____.

5. She is an artist who works with clay. Her _____ is pottery.

6. Bob has real _____ as a weaver.

7. Millions of people in that country don't have jobs. _____ is a serious problem.

8. When people can buy and sell a lot of goods, the _____ is in good condition.

9. Honda and Ford are companies that _____ cars.

10. The _____ destroyed many homes and highways.

**B**  In "Listening Focus," you will hear these expressions. Guess the meaning of the expressions and then discuss them with the class.

1. "Intangible cultural property" means _____.

   a. expensive crafts          b. rare talent that is disappearing

2. "Living national treasures" are people who _____.

   a. practice special unique crafts     b. work in a museum

# PRONUNCIATION FOCUS     *Syllable stress in multisyllable nouns*

In two-syllable nouns, the stress is usually on the first syllable.

   country          mountain

In nouns with three or four syllables, the stressed syllable varies.

   continent        democracy

However, in nouns that end in **tion/sion,** the syllable before **tion/sion** is usually stressed.

   situation        decision

**A  FIRST LISTENING**

• Read these words aloud.
• Listen and repeat the words.

   climate    location    island    forest    product    unemployment

**B  SECOND LISTENING**

• Read the following words aloud and guess which syllable is stressed. Underline the syllable.
• Listen to see if you underlined the right syllable in each word.
• Take turns saying the words with the correct stress to check your answers with the class.

| | | | |
|---|---|---|---|
| 1. ocean | 4. economy | 7. season | 10. museum |
| 2. population | 5. history | 8. industry | 11. talent |
| 3. desert | 6. culture | 9. government | 12. pottery |

**C  THIRD LISTENING: PAIR WORK**

• Read the conversation aloud and underline the stressed syllables in the nouns.
• Listen to check your answers. Then choose your part.
• Listen again and repeat your lines.
• Role-play the conversation.

George:  Maria, you're from Puerto Rico, aren't you?

Maria:   Yes, I am.

George:  Do you have four seasons?

Maria:   No, we have a tropical climate.

George:  What's the population?

Maria:   It's over three million.

George:  What is your main industry?

Maria:   Tourism. It's a beautiful island.

George:  Is your economy in good condition now?

Maria:   Yes. There's much less unemployment than before.

**A**  Before you listen to the conversation between an American and a Japanese, read the list of sentences below. Talk about any new vocabulary. Many, *but not all,* of the ideas are mentioned on the tape. Listen and check (✓) only the sentences that are true. Take turns with the class and talk about the main ideas.

___ Once the Winter Olympic Games were on the island of Hokkaido.

___ The other islands are Honshu and Kyushu.

___ There isn't much flat land in Japan.

___ Japan has a lot of earthquakes.

___ The city of Kobe had a big earthquake.

___ Kobe is a beautiful city to visit.

___ Most tourists want to visit Kyoto because it's beautiful and has so much history.

___ Japanese craftspeople make a lot of money.

___ Some of the most famous crafts are pottery, woodwork, and weaving.

___ What's special about the Japanese government is that it gives talented craftspeople money so they can continue their craft.

___ Many young Japanese are planning to practice a craft.

___ When only a few craftspeople are practicing a craft, the government gives the craft the title "intangible cultural property."

___ They keep "living national treasures" in an art museum.

**B**  Listen again and talk about these questions with your classmates.

1. Why are Japanese cities so crowded?

2. Why don't the Japanese pay much attention to most earthquakes?

3. Name one city other than Kobe or Kyoto mentioned in the conversation.

4. Which Japanese crafts does the American woman like?

# SPEAKING FOCUS     *Talking about countries*

**A**  Choose a country that you like or know a lot about. Draw a map of it in the box.

```
┌─────────────────────────────────────────────────────────┐
│                                                         │
│                                                         │
│                                                         │
│                                                         │
│                                                         │
│                                                         │
│                                                         │
└─────────────────────────────────────────────────────────┘
```

**GROUP WORK.** With three classmates, ask and tell each other about the country you have chosen. Include the following information.

EXAMPLE   *Is this country an island or on a continent?*

- if it is an island or on a continent
- what the climate is like
- how many seasons there are
- what the population is
- if most people live in the countryside or in towns or cities
- what your country produces and to whom your country exports its products
- what places are popular for tourists to visit and why
- what the economy is like right now

**B**  **GROUP WORK.** Talk about the attitude toward arts and crafts in your native country. (If you are from Japan, choose another country that you are familiar with.) Compare it to Japan. Are there any unique crafts, such as pottery and weaving, where you come from? Do you know of any famous artists or towns or villages where there are master craftspeople? Use an *Express!* question to ask about the meanings of new words.

Here are some arts and crafts that are common in different countries.

   jewelry     glasswork     rug making     basketry     embroidered clothing

## *Cross-Cultural Connection*

1. Find someone in the class who:                    **Student's name**
   - has visited a Spanish-speaking country      _____
   - has visited three different countries       _____
   - knows what the capital of Turkey is         _____
   - comes from a country that exports oil        _____
   - can name three cities in China              _____
2. Tell the class about the people you found.

# FOLLOW UP

**A** Choose a country (not your own) to research in the library or on the Internet. Give a two-minute talk. Choose interesting facts about this country. Bring maps, pictures of flags, or other material that will make your talk interesting. Use another paper for notes for your talk.

**B** **QUIZ: "NAME THE COUNTRY"**

Read the statements below and guess what country is being described. Write the name of the country on the line. Use an *Express!* question to ask about the meanings of any new words. Bring your answers to class and share them.

_____ 1. The people in this country speak Arabic. It is in Eastern Africa. In this country you can find the longest river in the world and the pyramids.

_____ 2. The people on this island continent speak English. When you go there you can see kangaroos and koalas.

_____ 3. There are 1.4 billion people in this country. It has the largest population of any country in the world.

_____ 4. The capital of this island country in the Caribbean Sea is Havana. The people there speak Spanish.

_____ 5. This country's shape is a peninsula. One of the cities is Pusan, a popular tourist resort.

_____ 6. There are more than 150 different languages in this country. Many college students use English, their second language, to communicate. New Delhi is a famous city.

_____ 7. The second longest river in the world, the Amazon, runs through this country in South America. A famous city there is Rio de Janeiro.

_____ 8. Most of this country is desert. The climate is hot all year. The most famous city is Mecca. It is a large country with a very small population.

**C** **A Perfect Country.** Use the map below to design a perfect country. Think about the following features and include them in your description of your "perfect" country. Then share your ideas with the class.

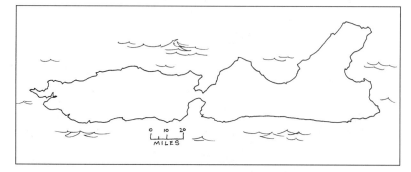

- where this country is located
- what the climate is like and how many seasons there are
- how many cities and towns it has and where most people live
- what the population is
- what the topography is like (mountains, beaches, forests, rivers)
- what main products and services there are
- what the economy is like

# 5 Get the Message!

## INTRODUCTION

1. _____

2. _____

3. _____

4. _____

5. _____

6. _____

**A**  **1 PAIR WORK.** Look at the pictures above and the words below. Match the pictures with the words and write the correct words under each picture.

| | | |
|---|---|---|
| laptop computer | videophone | fax machine |
| answering machine | cell phone | pager |

**2** Talk about these electronic machines.

EXAMPLE  *I use an answering machine . . .*

1. Which of these machines do you use? Explain why.

2. What are the advantages of a videophone over a cell phone?

3. Talk about other ways to communicate electronically.

**B**  **PAIR WORK.** When you phone a business, a school, a movie theater, or some-one's home, you often get a recorded message. Talk about the kinds of information you will hear when you call and get a recorded message from the following places.

EXAMPLE  *When you call a movie theater, you get information about . . .*

a movie theater       a museum       a library       a bus station

**A** **1 PAIR WORK.** Read the words and their meanings. Talk about anything you don't understand.

**Express!**

Practice these *Express!* questions. When you don't know what to do, or when you need help with an exercise, you can say: *Sorry, but I don't understand what to do. Which page are we on? Can you please help me with this EXERCISE?*

| | |
|---|---|
| **remind someone** | to tell someone to remember something |
| **dentist** | a doctor who fixes your teeth |
| **appointment** | a time and day you agree to meet |
| **Oldsmobile** | an American car |
| **pocketbook** | a handbag or purse women use to carry a wallet, papers, cosmetics |
| **wallet** | a flat folding case for holding paper money |
| **confirm** | to say something is correct |
| **pond** | a small lake |
| **strange** | unusual |
| **advantage** | a positive side to something |

**2** Complete the sentences with the correct words and talk about your answers. Take turns reading a sentence to check your answers with the class.

1. Jim likes to go fishing at a _____ near his house in the country.

2. I called my doctor to make an _____ for next Friday at four o'clock.

3. A Ford is an American car, and so is an _____.

4. When you have a problem with your teeth, you go to a _____.

5. An _____ of living in the city is that it is convenient to everything.

6. My dentist's secretary called to _____ me of my appointment on May 5.

7. I called the dentist's office back to _____ my appointment on May 5.

8. Lucy needs a larger _____ to carry all her papers and cosmetics.

9. Nancy needs a new _____ to carry her money and credit cards.

10. People with blue and pink hair look _____.

**B** **PAIR WORK.** Here are some messages that people left on answering machines. Talk about the messages and decide which are more formal and which are not formal. Who do you think left these messages? A friend? A family member? A business? Write "friend," "family," or "business" on each line. Then share your answers with the class.

EXAMPLE   *The first message is formal. A ... left it.*

**MESSAGES**

**First:**  Hello. This is Dana Downs from City Computers calling at

five o'clock on Wednesday, returning your call. _____

**Second:**  Polly, are you there? Pick up the phone! It's important!

_____

**Third:**  Hi, honey. Call me at the office as soon as possible. Bye.

_____

**Fourth:**  This message is for Joe. Please call Lee Rollins at 756-9080.

_____

**Fifth:**  Is this the DiCarlo residence? If it is, could Ronald call John at

985-0541 between noon and five today about his application.

Thank you. _____

**Sixth:**  It's me. It's seven o'clock, and I'm finally on my way home.

_____

To make the vowel sound as in *not,* open your lips, and with your tongue low in your mouth, drop your jaw.

To make the vowel sound as in *note,* make the letter *o* with your lips, and then close your lips slightly.

To make the vowel sound as in *out,* open your lips, drop your jaw, and then close your jaw.

## A  FIRST LISTENING

- Listen to the **vowel sound** in these words.
- Listen again and repeat.

| | | | | |
|---|---|---|---|---|
| hot | clock | John | doctor | office |
| road | home | show | phone | know |
| down | house | found | out | around |

## B  SECOND LISTENING: **PAIR WORK**

- Read the sentences below aloud.
- Listen to them and notice the vowel sounds in the words printed in **bold.**
- Write each word in bold on the line next to the word with the same vowel sound.
- Talk with the class about your answers. Then listen again to check them.

1. Do you **know how** much a **videophone** costs?

2. The boy **on** the **couch** is **watching** TV with the **sound so loud** you can hear it **outside** the **house.**

3. **Donna's phone** has a **low** dial **tone.**

4. I **stopped** at **Doctor** Bailey's **office.**

NOT _____

NOTE _____

OUT _____

## C  THIRD LISTENING: **PAIR WORK**

- Read the conversation silently. Choose your part and listen.
- Listen again and repeat your lines.
- Role-play the conversation.

John: Did you watch that TV show about the haunted house?

Joan: No, I was on the videophone till around ten.

John: Well, it was a great program. Now I believe in ghosts!

Joan: Oh, come on John! You didn't actually see one, did you?

John: No, but I just know they are out there!

Joan: Well, I've got to go. See you at one o'clock.

# LISTENING FOCUS    *Specific information; prediction; inference*

 **A**  Read the information in these messages on the answering machine. Listen to the messages. Listen again and write in the missing information. Then take turns reading the sentences to check your answers with the class.

### First Message

This message is from the _____ office.

Bonnie's appointment is for October _____ at _____ o'clock.

She has to call _____ to confirm.

### Second Message

She's calling at _____ o'clock.

She's working late at the _____.

She'll be home around _____.

### Third Message

John Jones at McBurger _____ is calling.

They found a brown _____.

The number to call is _____.

 **B**  Before you listen to two messages on the answering machine, read the sentences below. Listen to the messages and circle the correct answers. Then talk about your answers with the class.

EXAMPLE    *I think the person calling Mrs. Johnson is . . .*

### First Message

The person who is calling Mrs. Johnson is _____.
   a. her husband      b. the painter      c. the paint salesman

He's calling because he _____.
   a. is not sure about the color      b. can't finish today
   c. needs more money

### Second Message

The woman is calling her _____.
   a. mother      b. teacher      c. girlfriend

In high school the woman thought Don Dole was _____.
   a. strange      b. handsome      c. smart

 **C**  **PAIR WORK.** Listen again to the messages and decide what the missing endings are. Write them on the lines. Discuss your answers with your classmates.

### First Message

" . . . Well, if we don't hear back from you in the next hour or so, we'll just

finish up . . . uh . . . but it sure looks _____."

### Second Message

" . . . He sounds really nice now. He asked me _____."

**A** END THE MESSAGES!

**GROUP WORK.** Read these messages and talk about possible endings. Then share your answers with the class. Decide whose answers are the best.

EXAMPLE   *We think a good ending for the first message is . . .*
*This is our ending for the . . . message: . . .*

**First:**   Hello. This is the dog officer at the Boxford Dog Hospital. Do you own a large brown dog with white spots? I don't know how to tell you this, but we found . . .

**Second:**   Hi. Mom here. You'll never believe what happened to your father! Well, he got up at around four o'clock this morning to go fishing with his friends, hoping to get to the pond by six, but when he went into the garage . . .

**Third:**   This is Joe's Auto Body Shop calling, Connie. It's one o'clock, and we need to talk with you some more about your Oldsmobile. When we were taking it out for a test drive this morning, we . . .

**B** **PAIR WORK.** The following two messages were left on an answering machine. Read them and decide how you will answer them. Prepare what you will say, and role-play the conversations. Then role-play them to the class.

EXAMPLE   *Joan:   Hi, Mom. It's Joan.*
*Mom:   Oh, Joan! It's good to hear from . . .*
*Joan:   I'm sorry . . .*

**First Message**

Hi, Joan. It's Mom calling. You haven't called in a long time, and Dad and I are beginning to worry about you. Too bad you missed Dad's birthday last week. We don't live that far away, you know. I read in the paper that two students at your school were arrested for drunk driving. Is drinking a big problem at your college? Please call or e-mail us soon!

**Second Message**

Hi, Roger. It's me, Don. Hey, I know you're working part-time and going to school part-time. I'm thinking about doing the same thing. But I'd like to ask you about some things like how many hours a week you work and how many classes you have and . . . and do you have any time left for fun stuff? Call me back. OK?

## Cross-Cultural Connection

**GROUP WORK.** Talk about the following:

1. Answering machines are very popular in many countries. Is this true where you are from or where you live? Explain.

2. What are two advantages and disadvantages of communicating by phone and by e-mail to friends and family? Write them on the lines below. Then discuss them with your group.

   EXAMPLE   *One advantage of communicating by phone is . . .*

| | Advantages | Disadvantages |
|---|---|---|
| **Phone** | _____ | _____ |
| | _____ | _____ |
| **E-mail** | _____ | _____ |
| | _____ | _____ |

# FOLLOW UP

**A** Find the telephone numbers for two of the following places in your city with recorded messages. Call each place and write down the information. Tell the class what you learned.

**Movie Theater**
- what this week's movie is          _____
- what times it's playing             _____

**Museum**
- what days and hours it's open      _____
- what special exhibits are currently featured  _____

**Library**
- what days and hours it's open      _____
- if there's a special program for children  _____

**B** Call another student, a friend, or your teacher and leave a message on his or her answering machine. But first, prepare your message.

Your message:

_____

_____

Share your message with the class. If you received an answer to your message, tell the class what it was.

**G** **GROUP WORK.** There is a message on Shawn's answering machine that says, *"I'd love to come to your party on Saturday night. See you then. Bye!"* It's a man's voice, but it's not very clear, and Shawn doesn't know who it's from. The men he invited are described below. Decide which of them the message might be from and why. Write your notes on the lines. Discuss your opinions with the group.

EXAMPLE   *It could be Joe. Maybe he is feeling well enough to go to the party.*

Bob is going to be out of town for the weekend.

Morris is in town, but he's going to be at his friend's wedding all day on Saturday.

Joe is at home after breaking his left arm in a motorcycle accident.

Shawn is not sure when Ron's coming back from vacation in Ohio.

Don's phone has been disconnected because he didn't pay his bills.

Bozz is allergic to Shawn's two dogs.

Lonnie told Shawn that his parents are supposed to be visiting him either Saturday or Sunday.

Mo has to play in a baseball game Saturday night.

**Notes**

_____

_____

_____

_____

_____

# REVIEW    Units 1-5

## PRONUNCIATION

**A**  **1 GROUP WORK.** Read the message aloud to find the words with the **sh** sound as in *shop* and the **ch** sound as in *chop*. Write them on the correct lines. Practice the words that still give you trouble. Then read the words to your group.

> John, this is Sheila calling about Saturday. I showed the brochure with the information about the shore tour to Chuck. He found it interesting. He likes the beach and especially fishing. He wants to know when the boat leaves and how many hours it takes, as he gets off work around one o'clock. Also the cost. Joe says he's staying home to watch the college football championships. His phone number is 364-7289 if you want to call him. There's always a chance he'll change his mind. We should get this worked out now. We've only got two more days!

**Shop** _____

**Chop** _____

**2** Read the message again to find the words with vowel sounds as in *not, road,* and *down*. Write them on the lines. Practice the words that still give you trouble. Then read the words to your group.

**Not** _____

**Road** _____

**Down** _____

**B**  **PAIR WORK.** Underline the stressed syllables in nouns of two or more syllables in the following conversation. (If you have any difficulty, look at "Pronunciation Focus" in Unit 4.) Choose your part and practice the conversation.

A: Tell me more about the geography and climate of this island.

B: Well, there are some mountains in the middle and several rivers.

A: How about forests?

B: Oh, there are lots of forests. In fact, wood is one of the main industries and an important part of the economy.

A: And the climate?

B: The climate's perfect. The temperature never gets higher than 85° and never drops below 70°.

A: Sounds like a great place!

**C** **PAIR WORK.** Underline the stressed syllables in adjectives of two or more syllables in the following conversation. (If you have any difficulty, look at "Pronunciation Focus" in Unit 3.) Choose your part and practice the conversation.

A: Did you know that Belinda got married?

B: No, who did she marry?

A: Burt, a guy she met at work.

B: Oh, what's he like?

A: Tall, heavy build, with short, curly hair. Quite handsome. But I never liked the guy.

B: Why? What's wrong with him?

A: Lots of things. He's unfriendly, impatient, pretty irresponsible, unreliable, disorganized . . .

B: Wait a minute . . . Why did Belinda marry this guy?

A: Oh, she says he's very caring, compassionate, and romantic. And of course, she loves him!

# VOCABULARY

**A** **PAIR WORK.** Cross out the incorrect phrase or sentence. Choose your part and practice the conversation.

A: Why don't we do something this evening after work?

B:   a. I'll do something.              b. What do you have in mind?

A: I was thinking we could catch a late movie.

B:   a. I wasn't thinking.              b. Sounds good to me.

A: But I'd like something to eat before we go.

     a. How about you?              b. How are you?

B: Yeah, I'd like to eat first too.

A: Bundle up because the temperature's dropping to 30° tonight.

B:   a. Which bundle do you mean?     b. You've got to be kidding!

A: Shall we ask John to go with us?

B: No, he always likes to _____.

     a. do his own thing            b. make his own things

**B** PAIR WORK. Read the car ads and describe the cars. Then compare them. Include these words.

| | | |
|---|---|---|
| economical | reliable/dependable | comfortable |
| popular | expensive | |

| CADILLAC | TOYOTA |
|---|---|
| Black. Automatic. Excellent cond. CD and A/C. 25 m/g. $17,000. | White. Standard. V.G. cond. CD, no A/C. 35 m/g. $12,500. |

**C** GROUP WORK. Think of three people you know well. Write their names below. Use as many words as you can from the list to describe them to your group.

**Names:** _____ _____ _____

| | | | |
|---|---|---|---|
| sensible | sensitive/insensitive | kind | crabby |
| generous | patient/impatient | nosy | mean |
| talkative | organized | calm | bossy |
| nervous | impulsive | | |

**D** PAIR WORK. Complete the paragraph below with appropriate words from the list. Then take turns reading the sentences with the class.

| | | | |
|---|---|---|---|
| manufacturing | earthquakes | seasons | exports |
| unemployment | economy | tropical | |

This country has a _____ climate with only two _____:
the rainy season and the dry season. There are frequent, small
_____, but the people are used to them. There is very little
_____ in the country. The _____ is in good shape now.
The car industry is _____ more cars than last year. And it now
_____ twice as many cars as before.

**E** PAIR WORK. Write the letter of the phrase that completes each sentence beside the number. Read the sentences to the class.

EXAMPLE  *I reminded Jack . . .*

___ 1. I reminded Jack          a. some advantages and disadvantages.

___ 2. She used her cell phone to          b. but not her pocketbook.

___ 3. Someone stole her pager          c. and a positive side to most things.

___ 4. Living near a pond has          d. about his dentist appointment.

___ 5. There is a negative side          e. confirm her appointment.

Write two different questions to ask about the meaning of *CALENDAR*.

1. _____

2. _____

When you can't hear the teacher, you say: _____

_____

When you can't hear the tape, what do you say? _____

_____

If someone is speaking too fast for you to understand, what do you ask?

_____

If you didn't hear all of what a person is saying, what do you say? _____

_____

When you can't spell a word, you ask: _____

When you can't pronounce a word, you ask: _____

If you are lost in a lesson and don't know what to do, you say: _____

_____

If you need help with an exercise or activity, you ask: _____

_____

Check your answers with the class.

# CHECK YOUR PROGRESS

**A**  Is there any improvement in your skills?

|  | Listening | Speaking | Pronunciation |
|---|---|---|---|
| None | ☐ | ☐ | ☐ |
| Some | ☐ | ☐ | ☐ |
| A lot | ☐ | ☐ | ☐ |

**B**  I need to improve in ☐ ☐ ☐

**C**  What can you do to improve your skills? Answer the questions below.

|  | 1 | 2–4 | 5 | 6–8 | 9+ |
|---|---|---|---|---|---|
| 1. How many hours a week do you | | | | | |
| • spend in the language lab | ☐ | ☐ | ☐ | ☐ | ☐ |
| • listen to radio stations in English | ☐ | ☐ | ☐ | ☐ | ☐ |
| • watch English TV, videos, or movies | ☐ | ☐ | ☐ | ☐ | ☐ |
| • speak English with classmates outside of class | ☐ | ☐ | ☐ | ☐ | ☐ |
| • speak with English speakers | ☐ | ☐ | ☐ | ☐ | ☐ |

2. How many of these do you do each week in English?

- talk about your interests and pastime activities, like movies, sports, sight-seeing, etc. ☐

- ask a classmate to go with you to a movie, ballgame, etc. ☐

- ask friends about their weekend and tell them about yours ☐

- talk to friends about cars, bikes, or motorcycles, compare different makes, and say which ones you like ☐

- tell people what you or your family members are like ☐

- describe someone to a friend ☐

- talk about your country: its geography, climate, and economy, the products it exports, its arts and crafts, etc. ☐

- call a friend just to chat ☐

- call people and leave messages if they are out ☐

**D**  Look at your answers to Questions 1 and 2. Circle the things you are going to do to improve.

**E**  Talk with the class about your plan to improve. Your teacher can give you more ideas.

## INTRODUCTION

**A** **PAIR WORK.** Talk about the picture and the people in it. Find the meaning of the words below in the picture. Use the words to make sentences about the picture. Take turns telling your sentences to the class.

> EXAMPLE  *It's a picture of a . . .*
> *There are . . . people in a . . .   One is . . .*

| | | | |
|---|---|---|---|
| treadmill | fitness center | stair-climber | Walkman |
| leash | exercising | panting | exhausted |

**B** In English, there is an old saying: *Kill two birds with one stone.* This means to do two things at the same time to save time. Talk about all the things Marco, the man on the treadmill, is doing at the same time.

> EXAMPLE  *He's doing . . . things at the same time. He's . . .*

**C** Check (✓) which of these are important for your health. Tell the class.

> EXAMPLE  *I think . . . and . . . are very important for your health, but . . .*

___ having a lot of money      ___ doing a lot of exercise

___ eating large meals      ___ eating vegetables

___ getting a lot of sleep      ___ drinking wine

___ singing      ___ laughing

___ working      other: _____

**A** Find words or phrases in the list below that have similar meanings to the under-lined words in the sentences. To check your answers with the class, first read the sentence as written. Then read it again with the new word or phrase.

EXAMPLE    *John isn't in good shape. John isn't keeping fit.*

1. John isn't <u>in good shape</u>.                                    *keeping fit*

2. He has <u>put on</u> weight.                                    _____

3. He went to see a <u>diet specialist</u>.                  _____

4. She put him on a <u>low-calorie</u> diet.                _____

5. She wants him to <u>keep to</u> the diet.                _____

6. He said he <u>isn't into</u> exercise.                       _____

7. He wanted some <u>pills</u> to <u>take away</u> his headaches.    _____

_____

## Express!
Practice these *Express!* questions. When you don't know the answer, or when you are not sure of the answer to a question, you can ask: *What is the answer to NUMBER 5, please? Which is the correct answer to that question?*

| doesn't like | medicine | gained | get rid of |
| keeping fit | dietitian | follow | nonfattening |

**B**  **1 PAIR WORK.** Talk about the words in *italics* in the sentences below. To ex-pand on their meaning, complete the sentences with the correct words from the list. Then take turns reading the sentences to check your answers with the class.

EXAMPLE    *A calorie is a unit of energy in a . . .*

1. A *calorie* is a _____ in a food.

2. Sugar, bread, and _____ are examples of *carbohydrate* foods.

3. A *vegetarian* is a person who doesn't eat _____.

4. Examples of foods with *fats* are butter and _____.

5. Meat and _____ have a lot of *protein*.

6. We have big *muscles* in our arms and _____.

| meat | rice | poultry |
| legs | cream | unit of energy |

**2** Think of more examples of foods with protein, carbohydrates, and fats. Write them on the lines below and tell the class what they are.

EXAMPLE    *Other examples of foods with protein are . . .*

| Protein | Carbohydrates | Fats |
|---|---|---|
| _____ | _____ | _____ |
| _____ | _____ | _____ |
| _____ | _____ | _____ |

People understand you better when you stress the right words in a sentence. First, look at examples of words that are *not* usually stressed.

**Articles:** a, an, the          **Possessive adjectives:** my, his, your
**Prepositions:** to, of, in      **Conjunctions:** and, but, as
**Pronouns:** I, me, him

Now look at some words that *are* usually stressed. They are words that have important meaning in sentences.

**Verbs:** eat, jog                **Nouns:** tennis, muscles
**Adjectives:** good, sweet        **Adverbs:** regularly, daily
**Negatives:** can't, not          **Demonstratives:** that, these
***Wh-* question words:** what, which, why, who (and how)

## FIRST LISTENING: **PAIR WORK**

- Look at the stressed words in this conversation.
- Listen to the conversation. Then choose your part.
- Listen again and repeat your lines.
- Role-play the conversation.

> A: <u>Which</u> <u>sports</u> do you <u>like</u> to <u>play</u>?
>
> B: I <u>like</u> to <u>play</u> <u>tennis</u>, <u>baseball</u>, and <u>volleyball</u>.
>
> A: <u>Those</u> are <u>very</u> <u>energetic</u> <u>sports</u>.
>
> B: <u>Yes</u>. I'm <u>exhausted</u> after an <u>hour</u> of <u>tennis</u>.
>
> A: I <u>swim</u> and <u>walk</u>, and I <u>always</u> <u>ski</u> in the <u>winter</u>.
>
> B: <u>Skiing</u> must be a <u>lot</u> of <u>fun</u>!

## SECOND LISTENING: **PAIR WORK**

- Underline the stressed words in the conversation.
- Talk about your answers with the class. Then listen to check them.
- Choose your part. Listen and repeat your lines.
- Role-play the conversation.

> Daisy:  How many calories does a person need each day?
>
> Scott:  About eighteen hundred, I think. Why?
>
> Daisy:  I want to gain some weight.
>
> Scott:  Then you need more calories in your diet.
>
> Daisy:  Yes. About twenty-five hundred calories, I think.
>
> Scott:  Eat more carbohydrates and fats like cake and ice cream!
>
> Daisy:  I'm not really into sweet foods that much.
>
> Scott:  Well, you can eat a lot of bread and potatoes.

*Note: Be, have, do, will, would, shall, should, can, could, may, might, and must are usually unstressed unless they occur at the end of a sentence.*

**A**  **1**  Look at the sentences. Listen to the conversation between Henry, a college student, and the doctor. As you listen, check (✓) what you understand from their conversation.

___ Henry is very sick.

___ Henry's blood tests are fine.

___ He doesn't have any energy.

___ He has headaches all the time.

___ He has lost weight.

___ He has gained ten pounds.

___ He eats three meals a day.

___ The doctor wants Henry to eat more fries.

___ Henry's not into exercise.

___ The dietitian will give Henry a diet to follow.

___ Henry likes to play sports.

___ The doctor wants Henry to exercise four times a week.

___ Henry wants pills to give him energy and take away his headaches.

**2**  Listen again. Then take turns to give a gist of the conversation.

EXAMPLE   *Henry's tests are . . .   He has . . .*

**B**  Read the questions below. Then talk with the class about Henry and the doctor.

EXAMPLE   *I think the doctor is . . . with Henry because . . .*

1. Is the doctor patient with Henry? How do you know?

2. How does Henry feel about going on a diet?

3. What does he think about exercising four times a week?

4. Does he seem to like the doctor?

5. Which of these words would you use to describe Henry?

impatient     unfriendly     unhappy     crabby     bossy

## SPEAKING FOCUS   *Talking about exercise and diet*

**A** FITNESS QUIZ!

**GROUP WORK.** Talk about these statements. Write *T* for true or *F* for false on the line next to each statement. Take turns reading the sentences to discuss your answers with the class. Then ask your teacher which answers are correct.

EXAMPLE   *Walking five hours a week is not as good as jogging five hours a week is . . .   (true or false)*

---

\_\_\_ 1. Walking five hours a week is not as good as jogging five hours a week.

\_\_\_ 2. Carbohydrates give you more energy than fats.

\_\_\_ 3. Muscle is made up mostly of fat.

\_\_\_ 4. Low-fat and nonfat milk and yogurt have no protein in them.

\_\_\_ 5. Warm milk helps you to sleep.

\_\_\_ 6. It's best to eat a good meal half an hour before working out.

\_\_\_ 7. You should eat at least two servings (2 cups) of carbohydrate-based food (pasta, rice, cereal, bread, etc.) each day.

\_\_\_ 8. A good way to find out if you are at a healthy weight is to look in the mirror and see if you are shaped like an apple or a pear.

\_\_\_ 9. An example of a balanced meal is: beefsteak, 3 cups of rice, two rolls with butter, and vanilla ice cream.

\_\_\_ 10. Singing and laughing help to keep you in good health.

---

**B** **1 GROUP WORK.** Build your food pyramid! Look at the food groups below. If there is a food you don't like, you can replace it with another. For example: instead of "broccoli" you can put "squash." Decide which food group you should eat the most of each day and put it at the bottom of the pyramid. Put the food group you should eat the least of at the top.

**Food Groups**

**First:** beef, pork, chicken, turkey, fish, tofu, beans, eggs, nuts

**Second:** broccoli, spinach, green beans, corn, peas, carrots

**Third:** butter, cream, olive oil, sunflower oil

**Fourth:** bread, cereal, pasta, rice, potatoes

**Fifth:** cookies, cake, chocolate, candy, ice cream

**Sixth:** lettuce, tomato, cucumber, bean sprouts

**Seventh:** milk, yogurt, cheese, cottage cheese

**2** Compare your food pyramid with those of other groups. Explain which foods you would particularly recommend for each food group and why your pyramid is the best!

> EXAMPLE *We have put ... at the bottom of the pyramid ... For this group of foods we recommend ...*

**C** **GROUP WORK.** Circle the exercises or sports you do. Explain why you do them, how often you do them, where you do them, and how they help to keep you in good shape.

> EXAMPLE *I ... and I play ...*

| | | | |
|---|---|---|---|
| jog | run | skate | basketball |
| ski | tennis | football | other: _____ |

## Cross-Cultural Connection

**GROUP WORK.** What are some common foods or drinks in your culture? Write them on the lines. Tell your group which items you think are good for your health and why, and which are probably bad.

> EXAMPLE *We eat a lot of ... and ... I think ... is good for you because ...*

| Food and drink | Good for health | Probably bad |
|---|---|---|
| _____ | _____ | _____ |
| _____ | _____ | _____ |
| _____ | _____ | _____ |

**A** Design a low-calorie diet and exercise plan for a person who wants to lose weight. Ask your classmates what they think of it.

 EXAMPLE    *This is my plan. For breakfast . . .    Lunch will be . . .*

**DIET**

**Breakfast:** _____

**Lunch:** _____

**Dinner:** _____

**EXERCISE** _____

**B** What are the pros and cons (good and bad sides) of running as an exercise to keep in shape? Make a list of them. Then talk about them with your classmates. Do they agree with you?

 EXAMPLE    *I think the pros are . . .    And the cons . . .    What do you think?*

**Pros**   _____   _____   _____   _____

**Cons**   _____   _____   _____   _____

**C** Look at and read the pyramid about eating. Build a similar five-sentence pyramid about exercise. To help you read it with expression to your group, underline the words you will stress.

**Eating**

I eat pizza.

I like to eat pizza.

I like to eat mushroom pizza.

I like to eat a lot of mushroom pizza.

I like to eat a lot of hot mushroom pizza.

**Exercise**

I _____

_____

_____

_____

_____

# 7 What Are You Afraid Of?

## INTRODUCTION

**A** Look at the pictures and identify the words in the list. Use the words to describe the pictures and say what the people are afraid of.

EXAMPLE  *A man is jumping to one side on the sidewalk because . . .*

| | | | |
|---|---|---|---|
| flight attendant | heights | bulldog | oxygen |
| bank statement | spider | skyscraper | microphone |

**B** **GROUP WORK.** Which of the fears in the pictures (see the list below) do you think is the most common? Which is the least common? List the fears in order. Start with the most common and end with the least common.

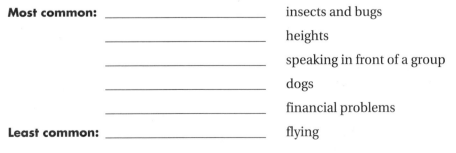

**Most common:** _____  insects and bugs

_____  heights

_____  speaking in front of a group

_____  dogs

_____  financial problems

**Least common:** _____  flying

Now ask members of your group about their lists. Tell them about yours.

EXAMPLE  *Which fear did you put first? I put . . . first.*

# LANGUAGE FOCUS    *Fear-related vocabulary*

**Express!**

Practice these *Express!* questions. When you want to know what the homework is or don't know how to do it, ask:

*What is the homework for today? Could you please explain the assignment to me?*

**A** Find the pictures that either match the words below or that show what they mean. Put the picture number next to each word. Check your answers with the class.

EXAMPLE   *There are . . . in the third picture . . .    The . . . picture shows death.*

___ snakes

___ loneliness

___ the dark

___ death

___ becoming homeless

___ deep water

___ losing a job

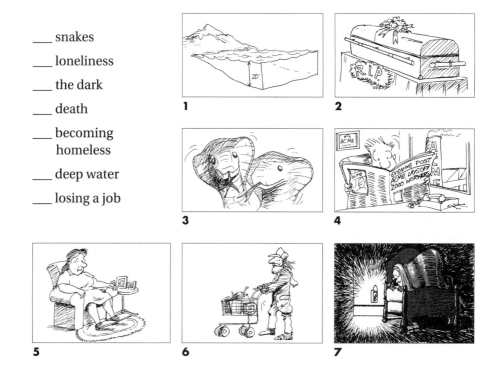

**B** Look at the expressions listed below. Which ones show the strongest feelings about snakes? Which ones show the mildest feelings? Discuss them with the class.

EXAMPLE   *I think . . . and . . . show the strongest feelings about snakes.*

hate snakes            terrified of snakes

afraid of snakes       can't stand snakes

petrified of snakes    scared of snakes

frightened of snakes

# PRONUNCIATION FOCUS    *Focus words*

In Unit 6, we looked at words that are usually **stressed** in a sentence. But sometimes, we give **extra stress** to words in a sentence to highlight, or **emphasize,** a particular **idea** or **feeling.**

## FIRST LISTENING: **PAIR WORK**

- Look at the conversation and the **stressed** words in boxes.
- Listen and notice the **extra stress** on these words.
- Choose your part. Listen and repeat your lines.
- Role-play the conversation.

> A: She's afraid of insects and 〔bugs〕.
>
> B: She's not just 〔afraid〕 of them. She's 〔terrified〕 of them.
>
> A: Right. But 〔he's〕 not afraid of insects and bugs.
>
> B: No, 〔he's〕 afraid of heights.
>
> A: How about 〔you?〕 Are 〔you〕 afraid of anything?
>
> B: 〔Nothing〕 that I can think of.

## SECOND LISTENING: **GROUP WORK (THREE PEOPLE)**

- Guess which word in each sentence should have **extra stress.**
- Draw a box around it and discuss your answers with the class.
- Listen to check your answers.
- Choose your part and role-play the conversation.

> Bob:    Let's watch the sunset from the top of the tower.
>
> Marge:  No, thank you. I'm petrified of heights.
>
> Bob:    Oh, yeah? Then let's go on a cruise to watch the sunset.
>
> Marge:  OK. Water doesn't bother me.
>
> Myles:  But it bothers me. I'm scared of deep water.
>
> Bob:    All right. Tell me what doesn't scare you two.
>
> Myles:  Flying doesn't scare us. We love flying!
>
> Bob:    Then we'll watch the sunset from a helicopter!

# LISTENING FOCUS    *Specific information; prediction*

 **A**    **1**  Look at the list of fears in the chart below. Use an *Express!* question to ask about any new words. Before you listen to a report on people's fears, guess the percentage of people who have each fear. Write the number in the first column. Then listen and write the percentage you hear in the second column.

| % | | |
| --- | --- | --- |
| Your Guess | Actual Percentage | Fear |
| | | speaking in front of a group |
| | | heights |
| | | financial problems |
| | | losing a job |
| | | becoming homeless |
| | | deep water |
| | | insects and bugs |
| | | sickness |
| | | death |
| | | flying |
| | | loneliness |
| | | dogs |
| | | driving or riding in a car |
| | | the dark |
| | | elevators |

 **2**  Listen again to check your answers. Tell the class how close your predictions were. Then take turns reporting about the fears.

> EXAMPLE    *My prediction for heights was . . . , which is pretty close!*
> *. . . percent were afraid of speaking in front of a group.*
> *. . . percent were terrified of . . .*

**B**    **GROUP WORK.** Talk about the following:

- what you find surprising about the report and why
- if you think some of the fears are more common in women
- if you think some of the fears are more common in men

> EXAMPLE    *I'm surprised to hear that . . .   I don't think some fears . . .*

## SPEAKING FOCUS    *Talking about fears*

**A**  GROUP GUESSING GAME

What are *you* afraid of? Write your fears on the lines below. The group can ask ten questions to find out what you are afraid of. If they can't guess what your fears are, you can tell them.

**Fears** _____  _____  _____  _____

> EXAMPLE    *Are you afraid of . . . ?*
> *No.*
> *Are you afraid of . . . ?*
> *Yes. I'm petrified of . . .*

**B** **1 GROUP WORK.** What can you do about fears? Think of suggestions to give Jim, Marlene, and Fabian. Write them on the lines.

| **Their Fears** | **What They Can Do** |
| --- | --- |
| Jim is terrified of exams. | _____ |
| Marlene can't stand people laughing at her English. | _____ |
| Fabian is petrified of losing his job. | _____ |

**2** Discuss your suggestions with the other groups. Decide on the most helpful suggestions for each person.

> EXAMPLE    *One thing Jim can do about exams is . . .    He can also . . .*

**C** **GROUP WORK.** Talk about particular fears that these age groups might have.

> EXAMPLE    *Children are often afraid of things like . . .*

children          adolescents (13 to 17)          young people (18 to 30)

---

 *Cross-Cultural Connection*

**GROUP WORK.** Do people in your culture have the same fears as Americans? Or are some of their fears different? Write their common fears on the lines. Discuss them with your group and give examples.

> EXAMPLE    *Many people are afraid of the same . . .    But a lot of people in my culture are also scared of . . .*

| **Same** | **Different** |
| --- | --- |
| _____ | _____ |
| _____ | _____ |
| _____ | _____ |

**A** Ask your friends or students in other classes about what they are afraid of. Write the information in the chart. Tell your group or class about their fears.

| Name | How he or she feels | Fear |
|------|--------------------|------|
| Janice | is scared of | financial problems. |
| | | |
| | | |
| | | |

**B** Prepare to talk about an experience when you were very scared (or someone you know was). Draw boxes around any words you will give extra stress to when telling your group about the experience.

EXAMPLE    *Once, I swam across a* huge *lake with a friend. In the middle of the lake, I thought about how* deep *the water was. I was* terrified *. My friend . . .*

**C** These geometric forms contain one or two words. Some words read clockwise (⤵), others read counterclockwise (⤴). Find the words and write them underneath. Read them to your class.

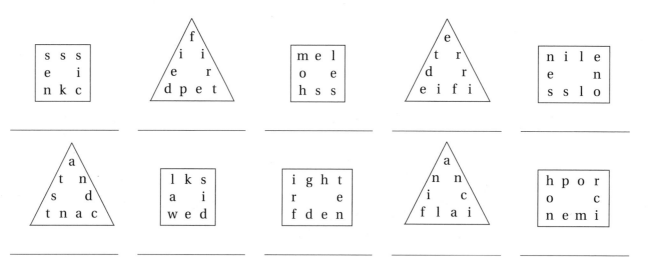

EXAMPLE    *The word in the first square is . . .*

## INTRODUCTION

**A**  Talk about the pictures with your classmates.

> EXAMPLE  *In the first picture, there are two young men in a . . .*
> *The driver looks very . . .*

**B**  Work with the class to tell the story in the cartoon. Begin like this:

> *Steve is driving a new sports car with his friend Nick. Steve looks very . . .*
> *Nick says . . .*

**C**  Decide which of the words below describe how Steve, Nick, and Steve's father feel after the car crash. If you don't know the meaning of a word or how to pronounce it, use an *Express!* question.

> EXAMPLE  *Steve must feel very . . . and . . .*

| | | | |
|---|---|---|---|
| shocked | annoyed | angry | guilty |
| miserable | embarrassed | ashamed | sorry |

**D**  What will Steve's father do when he hears about the accident? Share your opinion with the class.

> EXAMPLE  *I think Steve's father will . . .*

- warn Steve to drive more carefully
- loan his car to him again
- never trust Steve again
- punish him
- other: _____

# LANGUAGE FOCUS  *Warning expressions*

**Express!**

Practice these *Express!* questions. When you don't know the word for something you can see or can describe, ask:

*What is the word for that? (Point to it.) What do you call SIGNS THAT SAY THINGS LIKE "NO SMOKING"? How do you spell it?*

**A** **PAIR WORK.** Look at these warnings. Three of them have the same meaning. Decide which they are, what the others mean, and give examples of when you would use them. Then talk about your answers with the class.

EXAMPLE  *"Watch out!" means the same as ... and ...  You would use them when ...*

| | | | |
|---|---|---|---|
| Stop! | Look out! | Watch out! | Cool it! |
| Slow down! | Watch it! | Mind your step! | Careful! |

**B** **PAIR WORK.** These warnings are often used in situations where there may be a crime. Which ones match the pictures? Write them on the lines under the pictures. Then check your answers with the class.

EXAMPLE  *"Hands up!" and "..." match the ... picture.*

| | | |
|---|---|---|
| Hold it there! | Halt! | Freeze! |
| Hands up! | Don't move! | Hands in the air! |

_____  _____  _____

_____  _____  _____

**C** In "Listening Focus," you will hear these expressions. Write the letter of each meaning on the line. Then check your answers with the class.

EXAMPLE  *"Listen to the warnings" means ...*

___ 1. listen to the warnings

___ 2. loot [informal]

___ 3. the mystery was solved

___ 4. investigate

___ 5. tunnel

a. they found the answer to the problem

b. to look for the cause of a problem or situation

c. an underground passage

d. pay attention to the warnings

e. money

# PRONUNCIATION FOCUS     /ɪ/ hit   /iy/ heat

The back of your tongue touches both your top and bottom teeth when you make these vowel sounds. You blow a short puff of air to make the **short** vowel sound as in *hit*. You blow a long puff of air to make the **long** vowel sound as in *heat*.

## A  FIRST LISTENING

- Listen to the words with the **short** vowel sound in these sentences.
- Listen again and repeat the sentences.

> It is a big hill.
> This road is slippery.
> Dick didn't hit his sister.

- Listen to the words with the **long** vowel sound in these sentences.
- Listen again and repeat.

> She saw three thieves.
> He speeds on the freeway.
> The police seem to agree.

## B  SECOND LISTENING

- Listen and check (✓) the sentences you hear.
- Take turns reading the sentences to check your answers with the class.

| | |
|---|---|
| ___ This is a high hill. | ___ This is a high heel. |
| ___ She often slips when it's raining. | ___ She often sleeps when it's raining. |
| ___ The wick is almost gone. | ___ The week is almost gone. |
| ___ He bit the girl. | ___ He beat the girl. |
| ___ John can fill it. | ___ John can feel it. |
| ___ They are living now. | ___ They are leaving now. |

## C  THIRD LISTENING: **PAIR WORK**

- Read the conversation. Place a dot under the words with the **short** vowel sound as in *hit* and underline the words with the **long** vowel sound as in *heat*.
- Listen to the conversation to check your answers.
- Choose your part and role-play the conversation.

Nelly:  Did you read about the accident this week?

Dean:  You mean the one on the freeway?

Nelly:  Yes, near Green Hill, where a pickup hit a minivan.

Dean:  Yeah. It seems the guy didn't see the speed limit warning on the bridge.

Nelly:  And it was raining, so it was slippery.

Dean:  Uh-huh. But at least no one was killed.

**A** Look at the information about "The Story of the Week." Listen to the conversation and circle the words you hear to complete the story. Then work with the class to give a gist of the story.

> EXAMPLE *The story is from . . . It happened in . . .*

The story is from _____.
a. Romania          b. Australia          c. Argentina

It happened in _____.
a. a small city        b. a big city          c. the capital city

People heard _____ noises.
a. beating            b. digging            c. hitting

The people _____ the police.
a. warned            b. didn't warn

The police _____ to the warnings.
a. listened            b. didn't listen

The robbers got away with _____.
a. $25 thousand      b. $25 million        c. $25 billion

They dug a tunnel from _____ to the bank.
a. a house            b. an apartment        c. a store

This was the _____ tunnel bank robbery in six years.
a. twenty-fifth        b. fifty-fifth          c. seventy-fifth

**B** **PAIR WORK.** Read the questions. Listen again to the conversation and answer the questions. Talk about your answers. Then check them with the class.

> EXAMPLE *I know Jazz Themes is a . . . program because . . .*

1. Is *Jazz Themes* a TV or radio program? How do you know?

2. How long did it take to build the tunnel?

3. Jean says, "It sounds so easy." What does she think sounds easy?

4. At the end, Jim says, "Anyone know when the next plane leaves for Argentina?!" Why does he ask this? Why do they laugh?

**C** Draw the buildings on the downtown street. Include the bank, apartment building, tunnel, and other details from the story. Share your picture with the class.

# SPEAKING FOCUS    *Talking about warning expressions*

**A**  **GROUP WORK.** Talk about these warning signs and where you would find them. Compare your answers with other groups. Use an *Express!* question to find the meanings of new words.

EXAMPLE  *You'd find NO ALCOHOLIC BEVERAGES signs in . . .*

**B**  **PAIR WORK.** Talk about the warning expressions you would use for the situations below. Write them on the lines. Ask other pairs about their choices and decide which ones are suitable.

EXAMPLE  *I'd shout ". . ." to a person crossing the road . . .*
*What would you say to a thief . . .?*

- person crossing the road in front of a truck    _____
- a thief carrying away your TV    _____
- weak, old person nearing a deep bottom stair    _____
- three of your friends starting to fight    _____

**C**  ROAD PUZZLE!

**GROUP WORK.** Start in the empty space and move through the puzzle to find a legal parking place. You can move horizontally ( ↔ ) or vertically ( ↕ ), but you must follow the direction of all arrows. Tell your group about the route you followed and all the signs you passed.

EXAMPLE  *I followed the "One Way" arrow past the "Signal Ahead" sign.*
*Then I . . .*

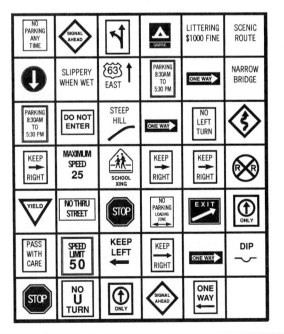

*Cross-Cultural Connection*

**GROUP WORK.** Talk about this old saying: *Better safe than sorry.*

1. What does it mean?
2. When would you use it?
3. Could you use it with driving?
4. Do you have a similar saying in your culture?

Think of three common warning signs in a country you are familiar with. Write them on the lines. Tell your group what they mean and where you find them.

_____

_____

_____

# FOLLOW UP

**A** Find as many warning signs as you can on the streets, in parks, and in public buildings. Make a list of them. Then share the information with the class. Use *Express!* questions to find the meanings of any warnings you don't understand, or don't know how to pronounce.

> EXAMPLE  *I found this warning, . . . , in the subway. I think it means . . .*

| **Warning** | **Where** |
|---|---|
| "Stand behind the yellow line." | subway platform |

**B** Go to a pharmacy or supermarket and find three products with warning labels. Ask your group or class about their products and warnings. Tell them about yours.

> EXAMPLE  *Which products did you find with warnings? What were the warnings? I found this warning on . . .*

| **Product** | **Warning** |
|---|---|
| _____ | _____ |
| _____ | _____ |
| _____ | _____ |

**C** Finish this story about Kim and Kathleen. Include as many of the words below as you can. Tell the story to your group or class.

| listen | taxi | thieves | see | warning | leave | hit |
|---|---|---|---|---|---|---|
| didn't | police | green | key | freeze | hill | mystery |

Kim and Kathleen were walking home from a party. When they reached their street, they . . .

## INTRODUCTION

**A** **PAIR WORK.** Look at the pictures and talk about the following.

EXAMPLE   *Lena wants to be a . . .*

1. What does Lena want to be? How many years do you have to go to law school after college graduation to get a law degree?
2. What does Peter want to be? Does he need to continue his education after high school?
3. What does Carla want to be? Does she need to continue her education after four years at the university?
4. What does Jason want to be? Many students are still undecided when they graduate from college. Talk about the reasons why.

**B** **PAIR WORK.** Look at the list of jobs and check (✓) the ones you think are the fastest growing and will be easy to find in the future. (You can write more jobs on the lines at the end of the list.) Talk about the reasons why you think so. Share your answers with the class. Use an *Express!* question to find the meanings of new words.

EXAMPLE   *I think a job as a nurse will be easy to find because . . .*

___ nurse     ___ preschool teacher  ___ home health aide

___ chef      ___ travel agent    ___ child care worker

___ legal secretary   ___ psychologist    ___ biochemist

___ software designer  ___ mail carrier    ___ auto mechanic

___ _____  ___ _____  ___ _____

# LANGUAGE FOCUS    *Career-related vocabulary*

**A**  **PAIR WORK.** Talk about the words below and their meanings. Complete the sentences with the correct words and check your answers. Then take turns reading the sentences with your classmates.

| | |
|---|---|
| **technical school** | a school that teaches people how to become mechanics, electricians, and so on |
| **goal** | something you plan and work toward; an aim |
| **retire** | to stop working, usually at the age of sixty-five |
| **Hollywood** | a famous place in California where movies are made |
| **competition** | a contest |
| **aspiring** | having a great desire to be something |
| **achieved** | finished successfully |

1. Fred is planning to quit his job and _____ to Florida.

2. I want to be a doctor. That is my _____.

3. Janet wants to go to Hollywood. She is an _____ actress.

4. Ken wants to go to _____ to learn how to be a mechanic.

5. _____ is a place for aspiring actors to go.

6. Lucy became a lawyer. She _____ her goal.

7. McDonald's and Burger King are in _____ with each other.

**B**  **PAIR WORK.** You will hear these expressions in "Listening Focus." Circle the meaning of each sentence. Read the sentences to check your answers with the class.

1. *I'm going to make it big* means "I'm going to be _____."
   a. rich and famous    b. happy and relaxed    c. a wild and crazy guy

2. *I'm going to give it my best shot* means "I'm going to _____."
   a. get shot    b. try hard    c. be successful

3. To *wait on tables* means to be a _____ in a restaurant.
   a. cook    b. waiter    c. manager

**C**  **PAIR WORK.** Talk about the meanings of these university degrees. Complete each sentence with the correct degree. Check your answers with the class.

| | |
|---|---|
| bachelor's degree | associate's degree |
| Ph.D. (doctor of philosophy) | master's degree |

You get an _____ when you graduate from a two-year college.

You get a _____ when you graduate from a four-year university.

You get a _____ when you study in your major for one or two years after your bachelor's degree.

You get a _____ when you study three to seven years in your major after your bachelor's degree.

# PRONUNCIATION FOCUS    *Selected reductions*

When Americans speak carefully, it is easy to understand them. When Americans speak quickly, or in a relaxed way, it is often difficult to understand them because their pronunciation changes. In relaxed English, some words are reduced and will sound quite different from the words that are spoken carefully.

**A**   FIRST LISTENING

- Listen to these examples. First, you will hear the **careful** English.
- Then you will hear **relaxed** or reduced English. (Relaxed or reduced English is only used when speaking, not writing!)

| Careful | Relaxed |
|---|---|
| 1. I'm going to go to college. | I'm "gonna" go to college. |
| 2. I don't know what I'll do. | I "dunno" what I'll do. |
| 3. I want to be a doctor. | I "wanna" be a doctor. |
| 4. We have to go now. | We "hafta" go now. |
| 5. What do you want to be? | "Whaddya" want to be? |
| 6. What do you want to do? | "Whaddya wanna" do? |
| 7. I've got to go now. | I've "gotta" go now. |
| 8. She has a lot of experience. | She has "alotta" experience. |

**B**   SECOND LISTENING

- Listen to the sentences. Some will be in **careful** English, and some will be in **relaxed** English.
- Listen again and decide which sentences are **careful** and which are **relaxed.** Circle the correct answers. The first one is done for you.

|  |  |  |  |
|---|---|---|---|
| 1. (careful)  relaxed | 5. careful  relaxed |
| 2. careful  relaxed | 6. careful  relaxed |
| 3. careful  relaxed | 7. careful  relaxed |
| 4. careful  relaxed | 8. careful  relaxed |

**C**   THIRD LISTENING: **PAIR WORK**

- Listen to the conversation. You will hear **relaxed** English.
- Listen again to the conversation and write the **careful** form for the relaxed speech you hear as you listen, or at the end.
- Check your answers. Then role-play the conversation.

John:  What are you _____ _____ do after you graduate, Mary?

Mary:  I _____ _____, but I _____ _____ decide soon.

John:  Yeah, I guess so. You don't have _____ _____ _____ time.

Mary:  And how about you? Do you _____ _____ be a businessman like your father?

John:  No, I'm _____ _____ be a doctor.

Mary:  Uh-huh. Well, I've _____ _____ go now. Bye.

**A** You will hear three conversations with people talking in relaxed English about their plans for the future. Read the first conversation. Then listen to it. Listen again and complete the sentences below as you listen or during the long pause at the end. Do the same with the other conversations.

### First Conversation

After high school, Paul is going to go to ___*technical*___ school.

At this school, he can learn how to be a _____ technician or programmer.

He wants to be an airplane _____.

He has to go to school there for _____ years.

After that he wants to get a job with an _____.

In a few years, he hopes to get married and buy a _____.

### Second Conversation

Judy and Bob have been working for _____ years.

They are going to retire in five years and move to _____.

They are going to spend the _____ in Florida.

Everyone will want to visit them in _____ or February.

They are going to buy a house with three _____ for all their visitors.

### Third Conversation

Karl wants to be an _____.

He's going to go to _____ and be famous.

He says, "I'm going to make it _____."

He says, "I'm going to give it my _____ shot."

**B** **PAIR WORK.** Talk about your answers. Then read a sentence each to check your answers with the class.

## SPEAKING FOCUS   *Talking about future plans*

**A** INTERVIEW

**GROUP WORK.** Walk around the class and ask three students these questions about their goals. Then report the information to your group.

1. What are your short-term goals in the next three to five years?

2. What are your long-term goals in the next five to ten years?

EXAMPLE   *I interviewed Carlo. First, he wants to improve his English so he can . . .*

| Name | Short-term Goals | Long-term Goals |
|---|---|---|
|  |  |  |
|  |  |  |
|  |  |  |

**B** **PAIR WORK.** Read these statements and decide if you agree or disagree. Give reasons. Share your ideas with the class. Use the following expressions to start some sentences.

I agree/disagree that        I don't know if        I think that

EXAMPLE   *I agree that . . .*

1. It's more important to make a lot of money than to like your job.

2. In the future, there will be no jobs for people who don't go to college.

3. It's important to make long-term plans for thirty years in the future.

4. The most important thing to consider when choosing a college is the tuition.

5. In the future, housewives will get salaries for their work at home.

*Cross-Cultural Connection*

**PAIR WORK.** Imagine these situations arising in your future plans. Can you think of any problems you might have? Talk about them. Then share them with the class.

EXAMPLE   *I think that marrying someone from . . .*

- marrying someone from a different culture
- living and working in a foreign country
- adopting children from a different country

**A** Interview two English-speaking people you know who are not in your class. Ask them about their hopes and dreams for the future. Use the following questions. Then share your findings with the class.

1. What do you think you'll be doing ten years from now?

2. Where do you think you'll be living? In what city? In what country?

3. What kind of job will you have?

4. Do you think you will be married or single?

5. How many children do you think you will have?

**B** Prepare a two-minute talk for your class. Choose *one* of the following topics.

1. In the future, do you plan to live in the city or the countryside? Explain your plan.

2. How are the elderly taken care of in your culture? What do you plan to do for your parents when they are elderly?

3. At what age do you think people will plan to retire in the future? Explain why.

**C** WORD PUZZLE

Find the eleven words from the list that complete the puzzle. Check your answers with the class.

EXAMPLE   *One across is . . .*

important
goal
shortterm
elderly
competition
degree
actor
chef
retire
nurse
countryside
relaxed
technical
agent
achieved

# 10 In the Future

**A** Talk with the class about what is happening in these pictures. Do you think these situations will be possible sometime in the future? If so, when do you think they will happen?

> EXAMPLE *People are waiting in line to board a . . . In the second picture, there's a . . .*

**B** **PAIR WORK.** Talk about how the discoveries and inventions below have changed our lives. What did we do before they were available? Then take turns and tell the class about one of them.

> EXAMPLE *I think that pop-top cans are great. Before we had them, we . . . Now we have Velcro, we don't need . . .*

| | | | |
|---|---|---|---|
| pop-top can | Velcro | vacuum cleaner | Post-its |
| washing machine | refrigerator | photocopying | hair dryer |

**C** Guess the number of years people have been doing the things listed below. Then talk about your guesses with the class.

> EXAMPLE *I think that people have been driving cars for about . . . years.*

- driving cars
- using computers
- traveling in space
- using antibiotics
- traveling by plane
- using answering machines

**A**  **PAIR WORK.** Talk about these words and their meanings. Complete the sentences below and check your answers. Then take turns reading the sentences to the class.

**Express!**

Practice these *Express!* questions. When you don't know the difference between two words or phrases, ask:

*What is the difference between BROUGHT UP and BROUGHT ABOUT? Could you please show me how to use them in sentences?*

| | |
|---|---|
| **cancer** | a disease in which cells of the body grow in an abnormal way |
| **cure** | something that brings back health; a medical treatment |
| **environment** | all of the surroundings and conditions in which we live |
| **pollute** | to make air, water, or soil harmful for people |
| **one billion** | 1,000,000,000 |
| **robot** | a machine that can move and do some of a person's work |
| **replace** | to change one person or thing for another |
| **batteries** | cells that give power to a flashlight or car motor, for example |
| **double** | twice the amount |
| **crops** | farm plants such as wheat, vegetables, and fruits |
| **bring up** | raise and care for a child as parents do |

1. Will doctors ever find a _____ for the common cold?

2. Bob has lung _____ because he smoked for forty years.

3. By recycling newspapers, we can save trees and help save the _____.

4. Mr. Rich makes _____ dollars every year. Wow!

5. I hope that someday a _____ will do my housework for me.

6. The number of students has increased. It's now _____ what it was last year.

7. For Jimmy's mechanical toy robot to work, it needs two _____.

8. There are many different kinds of _____ on that farm.

9. Robots can _____ people in many jobs.

10. Richard is a single parent. He has to _____ three children on his own.

11. Gases from cars and factories sometimes _____ the air.

**B**  Below are expressions we often use to talk about the future. Read the expressions and decide if they mean the near future or the far future. Put each expression under the correct heading. Then talk about your answers with the class.

EXAMPLE   *I think you use "sometime in the future" when you're talking about . . .*

| **Near Future** | **Far Future** |
|---|---|
| _____ | _____ |
| _____ | _____ |
| _____ | _____ |

| | | |
|---|---|---|
| sometime in the future | in a hundred years | one day |
| pretty soon | in a few years | shortly |

# PRONUNCIATION FOCUS  /l/ and /r/

When you pronounce **l,** the tip of your tongue touches your mouth just above the top teeth. When you pronounce **r,** both sides of your tongue touch your top teeth at the back.

**A**  FIRST LISTENING

- Listen to the **l** sound in these words.
- Listen again and repeat.

    late    collect    lead    people    alive    population    little

- Listen to the **r** sound in these words.
- Listen again and repeat.

    right    rot    true    computer    fewer    environment    robot

- Listen carefully to these pairs.
- Listen again and repeat each pair.

    light—right    collect—correct    cancel—cancer
    long—wrong    alive—arrive

**B**  SECOND LISTENING

- You will hear pairs of words.
- Listen and decide if the words are the same or different.
- Circle *same* or *different*, then check your answers with the class.

| | | | | | |
|---|---|---|---|---|---|
| 1. same | different | 4. same | different | 7. same | different |
| 2. same | different | 5. same | different | 8. same | different |
| 3. same | different | 6. same | different | 9. same | different |

**C**  THIRD LISTENING: **PAIR WORK**

- Read the conversation silently. Then choose your part and listen.
- Listen again and repeat your lines.
- Role-play the conversation.

Rosie:  What do you think people will look like in five hundred years?

Larry:  I think people will have little heads and be a lot fatter.

Rosie:  Little heads?

Larry:  Yeah. Computers will do all our thinking.

Rosie:  So . . . our brains will be smaller?

Larry:  Right, and our bodies will be a lot larger!

Rosie:  Oh boy, I sure hope you're wrong!

**A** You will listen to a conversation between Linda and Rick, who are talking about the future. Before you listen, read the sentences below and talk about any new vocabulary. Then listen and check (✓) the statements that are true. Take turns reading the true statements.

___ The world population now is five billion people.

___ The population is supposed to double in fifty years.

___ There is enough food now for ten billion people.

___ Scientists are always working to find new ways to raise crops.

___ Scientists have already discovered new kinds of food.

___ Linda is waiting for a little robot to do all her housework.

___ Linda will not be able to do all her shopping on the Internet.

___ Rick is going to buy an electric car.

___ Electric cars don't pollute the air.

___ Rick wants to go to the moon for a vacation.

___ Linda wants to go to the moon when there's a comfortable hotel there.

**B** **Who Said It?** Listen again and write "Linda" or "Rick" next to the quote. The first one is done for you. Talk about your answers with the class.

EXAMPLE   *Rick says, "Do you think there will . . ."*

___Rick___ "Do you think there will be enough food for ten billion people?"

_____ "They'll probably discover new kinds of food."

_____ "I'm waiting for a little robot to do all my housework!"

_____ "Pretty soon, you won't need to go to the mall."

_____ "Speaking of saving, what I'd like to do is try to save the environment."

_____ "But you can only drive a short distance and then you have to recharge the batteries."

_____ "Sure, I'd go to the moon."

_____ "You won't be leaving on that trip for a long time!"

# SPEAKING FOCUS     *Predicting the future*

**A** **PAIR WORK.** Here is a list of possible future happenings. Talk about these events and decide if they will:

| | |
|---|---|
| happen pretty soon | happen sometime in the future |
| probably happen one day | will never happen |

Then share your ideas with the class. Explain why you think these events will or will not happen.

EXAMPLE     *I don't think we will ever travel to the moon . . .*
*Yes, I think pretty soon . . .*
*I think . . . sometime in the future.*

1. We will travel to the moon for a weekend.

2. Computers will replace teachers.

3. We will work only three days a week.

4. There will be peace everywhere in the world.

5. Fish farms will replace ocean fishing.

6. People from outer space will visit us.

7. Doctors will find a cure for every kind of cancer.

8. (Add one more idea of your own.) _____

**B** **GROUP WORK.** Some scientists think we may have the following devices one day. Talk about them and say what you think. Mention all the ways they would improve your life. Share your views with the class.

EXAMPLE     *An Assemblo-tron would be a great device. You wouldn't have to . . .*
*or . . .*

1. Assemblo-tron: a device that looks like a small microwave oven with tubes at the back that go to the city's Department of Food. It will have a keyboard with favorite foods. If you want steak, fries, and salad, you hit the F4 button and in a few seconds your meal will arrive! When you finish eating, the device will disassemble the plate, knife, and fork.

2. A tiny medical robot will be put in your bloodstream. It will kill viruses and cancers and will keep you healthy all the time.

**C**  **PAIR WORK.** Here is an ad for a future business. Read the ad and talk about the following:

1. Would you like your children to be brought up by "professional parents"?

2. What would some of the advantages and disadvantages be?

EXAMPLE  *One advantage of having professional parents is . . .   However, a disadvantage is . . .*

---

## DON'T WORRY ABOUT PARENTHOOD!

We'll bring up your children and make them into
responsible, successful adults.

---

- *Excellent food and education*        *• Just visit your children once a week*
- *Minimum five-year contracts*

---

*Cross-Cultural Connection*

**GROUP WORK (THREE PEOPLE).** Pretend you are very rich. Choose a country to which you would like to donate $3 million for research. Choose three fields of scientific research and divide the money between them. Explain your plan to the group and tell why you would support this research.

EXAMPLE  *One field of scientific research that is important is . . .   I would donate . . .*

|  | First | Second | Third |
|---|---|---|---|
| **Field** |  |  |  |
| **Amount** |  |  |  |

**70**    SO TO SPEAK 2

# FOLLOW UP

**A** Go to the library or use the Internet to find out about two recent inventions or discoveries. Make some notes and report on them to your class.

| Name of Invention | What It Is | What It Is For |
|---|---|---|
|  |  |  |
|  |  |  |
|  |  |  |

**B** A new invention! What do you think needs to be discovered or invented to improve our well-being? Explain why. Describe or draw your invention and share it with your class.

EXAMPLE *One thing I think needs to be discovered is . . .*

**C** How much do the items below cost now? How much will they cost in the future? If you are not sure how much these items cost now, use the newspaper or Internet to find out. Then try to predict how much they will cost ten years from now. Write the prices in the blank spaces. Compare your answers with others in the class.

|  | **Now** | **In Ten Years** |
|---|---|---|
| a cup of coffee | _____ | _____ |
| an ESL textbook | _____ | _____ |
| a can of soda | _____ | _____ |
| a small Toyota | _____ | _____ |
| a cell phone | _____ | _____ |
| a Walkman | _____ | _____ |
| a month's rent for a studio apartment | _____ | _____ |
| an ice cream cone | _____ | _____ |
| a movie ticket | _____ | _____ |
| a year's tuition at this school | _____ | _____ |

# PRONUNCIATION

**A**  **GROUP WORK.** Find words in the paragraph below that have the same vowel sounds as in *bit* and *beat*. Write the words on the lines. Then practice the words and read the paragraph to your group.

**Bit** _____

**Beat** _____

While Dean is driving to work, he sees a policeman stopping a green car speeding on the street leading to the freeway. Just as the policeman is giving the man a ticket, a thief leaps in front of him carrying a big TV.

**B**  **PAIR WORK.** Underline the stressed words and draw a box around the word that has **extra** stress in each sentence. (See Units 6 and 7 if you need help.) Check your answers with the class. Then role-play the conversation.

A:  Sara spends hours exercising every day.

B:  Well, she's so afraid of getting sick.

A:  Yes, but just one hour of exercise is enough.

B:  True. I never exercise for more than one hour.

A:  Uh-huh. But you are not afraid of getting sick.

B:  No, but I'm scared of other things!

A:  I'm sure everyone is scared of something.

**C**  **PAIR WORK.** Look at the relaxed, or reduced, forms used in this conversation. Write the careful, or long, forms on the lines. Role-play the conversation with the careful forms.

A:  Whaddya wanna do tonight?

B:  Study. I hafta write a paper.

A:  I'm gonna watch the ball game.

B:  I've gotta go. I've a lotta stuff to do.

A:  _____
    do tonight?

B:  Study. I _____
    write a paper.

A:  I'm _____
    watch the ball game.

B:  I've _____ go.
    I've a _____
    stuff to do.

**D**  **GROUP WORK.** Practice reading this poem to your group. Then ask the class if they think what the poem says is right or wrong.

If you live right,
Your future will be bright.
If you live wrong,
you'll not survive for long.

**A** **GROUP WORK (THREE PEOPLE).** Talk about the meanings of the expressions in the list. Complete the conversation with the correct expressions. Role-play the conversation.

| brought up | in good shape | put on | not into |
|---|---|---|---|
| cool it | can't stand | slow down | watch out |

Lori:   Hey, Gene! _____ for that man!

Gene:  Okay. . . _____, Lori! I saw the guy crossing the street.

Ann:   The fitness center is on the next block. Can you _____?

Gene:  Sure. But you don't need to exercise. You're _____.

Ann:   Yeah. But I don't want to _____ weight.

        I _____ being fat!

Lori:   I'm _____ fitness centers, but I do a lot of sports.

Gene:  Me, too. I was _____ by my father, and he was into all

        kinds of sports.

**B** **1 PAIR WORK.** There are fourteen words from the last five units in the puzzle. Find as many as you can and circle them. Words read from left to right, from right to left, from top to bottom, and from bottom to top.

| x | p | r | o | t | e | i | n | x | p |
|---|---|---|---|---|---|---|---|---|---|
| z | e | y | v | e | l | c | r | o | e |
| s | m | d | i | o | v | a | t | p | t |
| e | b | g | o | a | l | c | o | r | r |
| k | a | s | p | o | r | c | r | l | i |
| a | r | f | r | e | e | z | e | l | f |
| n | r | r | e | c | n | a | c | u | i |
| s | a | j | h | a | l | t | k | t | e |
| u | s | e | r | i | t | e | r | e | d |
| s | s | g | n | i | r | i | p | s | a |

**2** Work with the class to put the words on the board. Take turns and make up sentences with the words.

# Express! QUESTIONS

When you don't know the answer, or when you are not sure of the correct answer to a question, what can you ask?

1. _____

2. _____

When you want to know what the homework is, or don't know how to do it, you can ask:

1. _____

2. _____

When you don't know the word for something you can see, what can you ask?

_____

When you don't know the word for something you can describe, what do you say?

_____

When you want to open or close the window, you can say:

1. _____

2. _____

3. _____

When you don't know the difference between two words or phrases, you can ask:

1. _____

2. _____

## CHECK YOUR PROGRESS

**A**  Is there any improvement in your skills?

|  | Listening | Speaking | Pronunciation |
|---|---|---|---|
| None | ☐ | ☐ | ☐ |
| Some | ☐ | ☐ | ☐ |
| A lot | ☐ | ☐ | ☐ |

**B**  I need to improve in      ☐      ☐      ☐

**C**  What can you do to improve your skills? Here are some ideas.

- Join a sports club and talk about sports you like to play or watch. Talk about sports stars and compare games or teams. Volunteer to play on a team. Go walking with friends and talk about outdoor activities.

- Talk with friends about healthy diets. Ask them which foods they think are healthy.

- Talk with friends or family members about fears. Ask them what their greatest fears are. Tell them about your fears and what you do about them.

- Point out warning signs to your classmates. Tell your friends the story about the bank robbery you heard on tape in Unit 8 and about how the police didn't listen to the warnings. Or talk about another story in which someone didn't listen to a warning.

- Ask students and friends what their plans for the future are and what kinds of jobs and salaries they hope to get. Ask them if they want to get married and have children and where they would like to live. Ask them to explain why.

- Talk to people about what the future will be like: How different will lifestyles be? Will robots be doing the work that people do now? How will transportation change? Will scientists find more cures for diseases? Will people live longer? Tell them what you think.

**D**  What else can you do to improve?

_____

**E**  Talk with your class and the teacher about your plan to improve. Ask your teacher for more suggestions.

# 11 Have You Heard the News?

## INTRODUCTION

**A** Talk about the pictures with the class.

1. Where are the people?

2. What are they doing?

3. Which of the words below best describes how each person looks?

4. Why do you think they look like this?

> EXAMPLE *The man is watching TV at home... He looks... Maybe the news story is about something...*

| amused | surprised | shocked | interested | worried | horrified |

**B** **PAIR WORK.** Look at the headline about the balloonists. Where do you think they were going and why? What went wrong? Imagine their story. Then share it with the class.

> EXAMPLE *We think the balloonists were trying to go...*

**C** **GROUP WORK.** Check (✓) all of the types of news that you are interested in. Ask your group about the news they are interested in, where they get it, and how often.

> EXAMPLE *Which news are you interested in?*
> *Well, I'm interested in... and... and also...*

\_\_\_ international    \_\_\_ national    \_\_\_ local

\_\_\_ political    \_\_\_ financial    \_\_\_ crime

\_\_\_ sports    \_\_\_ science    \_\_\_ arts

\_\_\_ entertainment    \_\_\_ fashion    other: _____

**A**    **1 GROUP WORK.** Match the words in the list with the pictures below. Write the correct word on each line. Check your answers with the class.

**Express!**

Practice this *Express!* question. When you don't understand a question or an answer, you can interrupt and say:

*Excuse me for interrupting, but I don't understand the QUESTION/ANSWER. Would you please explain it again?*

| tornado | floods | earthquake | hurricane |

_____    _____

_____    _____

**2** Now talk about these natural disasters. In which parts of the world do they often happen? Have you ever experienced any of them? Describe the disaster and say what happened.

EXAMPLE    *I was once in a . . .    When it happened, I was . . .*

**B** **GROUP WORK.** These words are often used with natural disasters. Decide on their meanings. Take turns telling your answers to check them with the class.

EXAMPLE *A disaster is a situation with a lot of destruction. "Damage" means . . .*

1. _d_ disaster          a. hurt or harmed
2. ___ damage           b. very bad
3. ___ destroyed        c. die in a violent way
4. ___ severe           d. a situation with a lot of destruction
5. ___ be killed        e. taken from a dangerous place to safety
6. ___ injured          f. harm to a person or thing, like buildings
7. ___ rescued          g. made something happen
8. ___ caused           h. completely broken or spoiled

**C** **GROUP WORK.** You will hear the words below in "Listening Focus." Talk about them and their meanings. Make up sentences with these words and share them with the class.

EXAMPLE *My aunt has arthritis.*

| | |
|---|---|
| **arthritis** | a disease of the joints of the body |
| **eliminate** | to get rid of; to remove |
| **poverty** | the state of being poor |
| **unemployment** | a situation where people cannot find work |
| **python** | a dangerous snake |
| **smuggler** | a person who brings something into a country illegally |
| **beat** | to win in a sports game |
| **octuplets** | eight babies born at the same time to one mother |

As shown in Unit 7, we often give **extra stress** to words to emphasize an idea or feeling. In natural conversation, we often use different kinds of **focus** words. Some may emphasize ideas or new information; others may emphasize feelings or clarify meaning.

### A  FIRST LISTENING: **PAIR WORK**

- Look at the **focus** words in this conversation.
- Listen to the conversation. Then choose your part.
- Repeat your lines with the tape. Then role-play the conversation.

> A: I've just received some $\boxed{\text{bad}}$ news.
>
> B: You mean about the $\boxed{\text{test}}$ yesterday?
>
> A: Yes, I $\boxed{\text{failed}}$ the test.
>
> B: Me $\boxed{\text{too}}$, but we can take it again next week.

### B  SECOND LISTENING: **PAIR WORK**

- Listen to the conversation. Then draw boxes around the **focus** words.
- Talk about your answers with the class.
- Listen to check your answers. Then role-play the conversation.

> A: I heard about the tornado on the radio.
>
> B: Which tornado?
>
> A: The one in Texas.
>
> B: Was it as bad as the one in Louisiana?
>
> A: It was much worse. A hundred people were killed.
>
> B: That's twice as many people!

### C  THIRD LISTENING: **PAIR WORK**

- Look at the picture and guess what news Lisa is telling her friend. Write the new information words in the blank spaces.
- Draw boxes around the words you think Bill emphasizes.
- Listen to check your answers. Then role-play the conversation.

> Lisa: Chuck and I got _____ last Saturday!
>
> Bill:  Well, congratulations!
>
> Lisa: Thanks. And we've _____ to another apartment.
>
> Bill:  Boy, you have been busy!
>
> Lisa: Oh, and I won a _____ in the ski competition!
>
> Bill:  Wow!
>
> Lisa: And I also _____ my term paper.
>
> Bill:  Great! I haven't even started mine.

## LISTENING FOCUS   *Summary of main ideas; details*

 **A**   **1** Read the sentences and try to imagine what the complete idea is. Use an *Express!* question to ask about any new words. You will hear a TV newscast. Listen for the main ideas in the news stories. On each line, write the word that completes the main idea.

| News Item | Main Idea in News Story |
|---|---|
| **First** | There was a terrible _____ in Florida. |
| **Second** | There were bad _____ in the Midwest. |
| **Third** | A smuggler tried to smuggle a large _____ into the country. |
| **Fourth** | The United Nations Secretary General wants international help to eliminate _____ poverty. |
| **Fifth** | The government said the U.S. economy is _____ than ever. |
| **Sixth** | Japan got the _____ medal in ski jumping. |
| **Seventh** | The Lakers beat the Celtics 120 to _____. |
| **Eighth** | A new _____ will help pets with arthritis. |

**2** Take turns reading the sentences to summarize the main ideas in the news stories.

 **B**   **PAIR WORK.** Read the questions. Listen to the newscast again and find as many details as you can about the stories. Talk about the stories with your partner. Then share the details you found with the class.

EXAMPLE   *. . . people lost their lives in the tornado. Homes were . . .*

1. How many people lost their lives in the tornado?

2. What happened to the homes?

3. How many people lost their lives in the floods?

4. How many families were rescued?

5. How did the smuggler smuggle the python?

6. When does the Security Council meet to discuss world poverty?

7. What does the government say about unemployment?

8. Which country got the silver medal in ski jumping?

## SPEAKING FOCUS    *Talking about the news*

**A**  **1 GROUP WORK.** Look at the beginnings of the news stories below. Choose three and make up stories to complete them.

Police are looking for a . . .          The United Nations is . . .

In medical news, a cure for . . .       A new pop group called . . .

There was an earthquake of 6.8 . . .    A panda was born . . .

**2** Share your stories with the class.

**B**  CLASS NEWSCAST

**GROUP WORK.** Decide with the class which news category in the list each group will report on. Prepare your news and write it on the lines below. Then decide who will tell each part. Emphasize new information when you tell your news to the class.

EXAMPLE  *In sports news, . . . won the . . .   Scientists have . . .*

sports              fashion

science             crime

arts                education

politics            business

entertainment       general interest

_____

_____

_____

_____

_____

**C**  **GROUP WORK.** Talk to the class about important or interesting news about your school, company, or family. Are you happy, shocked, surprised, or concerned about it?

EXAMPLE  *I've heard that my company . . .   I'm concerned . . .*
*I have good news from my family. My . . .   I'm very happy . . .*

## Cross-Cultural Connection

INTERNATIONAL NEWS! **GROUP WORK.** Choose a country to report on. Think of three news stories from this country to tell your group. Make notes about them on the lines. Then share your stories with the class.

EXAMPLE    *The most interesting news from . . . is . . .*
*Another news story is . . .*

_____

_____

_____

# FOLLOW UP

**A**    Watch the news on TV. Find one funny piece of news, one amazing news item, and one terrible news story. Talk about them with your group or class.

EXAMPLE    *What did you hear on the news?*
*I heard an amazing story about . . .*

**B**    SURVEY

Ask four friends or students in other classes if they are interested in the news. Report your findings to your group or class.

EXAMPLE    *One person said he never gets the news because he . . .*
*Two people said . . .*

| Question | First Person | Second Person | Third Person | Fourth Person |
|---|---|---|---|---|
| How often do you listen to or read the news (every day, twice a week, never)? | | | | |
| Where do you get the news from (radio, TV, newspaper, Internet, friends)? | | | | |
| What kinds of news are you interested in (crime, sports, politics, entertainment, etc.)? | | | | |

**C** CROSSWORD

Some of the words in the puzzle are names of natural disasters. Other words are often used with stories of natural disasters. Find as many as you can. Work with the class to put all the words on the board and take turns reading them.

**Across**

3. A situation with a lot of destruction.
4. This shakes the ground and buildings.
7. Past tense of *lose*.
8. Too much water on the ground and even in buildings.
10. Word used to describe very bad damage.
11. The hurricane _____ terrible damage.
12. Saved from a dangerous situation.

**Down**

1. Storms can _____ buildings.
2. A sudden, fast, twisting storm.
5. Completely broken or spoiled.
6. When people lose their lives, they are _____.
7. Word for more than one *life*.
9. Hurt or harmed.

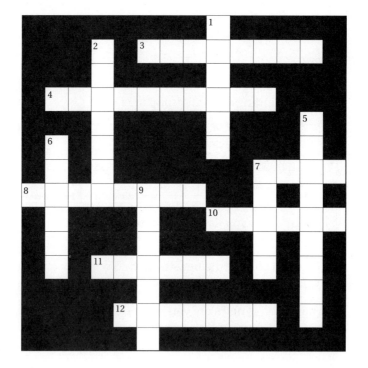

# 12 Are You Telling the Truth?

## INTRODUCTION

**A** Talk about and describe the pictures with your classmates. Use an *Express!* question to ask about new words.

1. Where are the people?

2. What do you think is happening?

3. What do you think the people are saying?

4. How do you think they feel?

| | | | |
|---|---|---|---|
| sorry | pleased | happy | worried |
| guilty | skeptical | angry | suspicious |

EXAMPLE  *The girl in the first picture is about seventeen years old. She's wearing . . .  She's in . . . because she probably . . .  I think she feels . . .*

**B** **PAIR WORK.** Find the correct lines for each person and write them in the balloons. Role-play the conversations to see if they sound correct. Check with the class.

EXAMPLE  *The girl says . . . and the principal says . . .*

Yes, honey. I had an important meeting tonight.

I'll check to see what time the bus driver came by your street.

I promise to cut taxes 30 percent this year.

Don't tell me you've been working late at the office!

I was late because the school bus came early and I had to walk.

You said that last year, and you didn't. How can we trust you?

**C** Do you think the girl, the husband, and the politician are telling the truth? Explain your answers.

EXAMPLE  *I think the girl . . .  I'm sure the . . .*

# LANGUAGE FOCUS   *Topic-related vocabulary*

**Express!**

Practice these *Express!* questions. When you need to talk to the teacher after class, you can say:

Can I talk to you for a moment after class about the ASSIGNMENT?

I have something to ask you. Can I make an appointment to see you? I need to talk to you about . . .

**A**   **PAIR WORK.** Read the paragraph about Sonia and Tom. The italicized words are used in this unit. Find the correct word for each meaning below and write it on the line next to it.

Sonia bumped into an old boyfriend on her way home from work. They went for a coffee and chatted. She told Tom, her husband, that she had to work late because she wanted to *protect* him. But she felt *guilty* about it. Tom was *skeptical* about her excuse. The next morning, Sonia was very quiet and Tom became *suspicious:* he thought she had lied to him. Sonia realized that if it happened again, Tom would lose *trust* in her and it would affect their *relationship*.

1. _____suspicious_____ feeling that something is strange or wrong
2. _____ a close, loving friendship
3. _____ feeling bad after doing something wrong
4. _____ complete belief in someone
5. _____ to keep from hurt or harm
6. _____ feeling unsure that something is true

Now check your answers with the class.

EXAMPLE   *"Suspicious" is feeling that something is strange or wrong.*

**B**   **PAIR WORK.** These expressions are also in this unit. Talk about the expressions and complete the sentences with the correct ones. Take turns reading the sentences with the class to check your answers.

| social skills | cheat on | ran a red light | turn in |
|---|---|---|---|

1. The teacher asked the students to _____ the book report on Monday.

2. Adrian _____ and was hit by a truck.

3. Your _____ are good if you communicate easily and say the right things.

4. Roger doesn't usually _____ his girlfriend, but last week I saw him kissing Sara at a party.

# PRONUNCIATION FOCUS    *Rhythm*

Rhythm in language is like the rhythm, or beat, in music. The strong, regular beats of English fall on the **stressed** words in a sentence. (See Unit 6 for a review of sentence stress.)

**A** FIRST LISTENING

- The dots show the rhythm, or beat. Listen and tap your finger to the beat.
- Listen again and read the sentences with the tape.

He talked to Clive about telling the truth.

He told him never to lie.

Clive didn't realize he had lied about anything.

**B** SECOND LISTENING: **PAIR WORK**

- Listen, and tap the beat in the lines.
- Listen again and repeat. Place a dot above the words with the beat.
- Read the lines while your partner taps the rhythm.

People should always tell the truth.
This is what parents teach us.
And this is what teachers say.
Then why do we sometimes lie?

**C** THIRD LISTENING: **PAIR WORK**

- Read the lines and tap the rhythm.
- Place dots over the words with the beat.
- Listen to check your answers.
- Choose your part and role-play the conversation.

Student:  I didn't know the exam was on Tuesday.

Teacher:  But I wrote it on the board.

Student:  Then I guess I completely forgot.

Teacher:  There was no excuse for forgetting.

Student:  I know. What can I do about it now?

Teacher:  Nothing. You'll just have to repeat the course!

**A** **1** You will hear a talk about research on lying done by Dr. Leonard Saxe. First, read the summary of the main ideas below. Try to predict some of the missing words. Then listen and complete the summary with the words you hear.

Our parents and teachers tell us that _____ is bad. They _____ us when we lie. Dr. Leonard Saxe and other psychologists say that lying is a social _____. Sometimes we lie to protect ourselves. Sometimes we lie to protect other people because we don't want to _____ them by telling the truth.

Saxe did a study on lying in relationships with _____ graduate students. More than _____ percent of them said they lied, and almost all said they lied because they did not want to hurt their

_____.

Saxe did another study on lying to _____. When students did not _____ a paper on time to the professor and the paper was important for their final grade, many of the students _____ in their excuses. The professor gave students with good _____, like being sick with the flu, more time to write the paper. But the students who told the professor they had no excuse did _____ get more time. Afterward, those students who said they had no excuse—in other words, the students who told the _____—were sorry they did not lie to the professor because they got _____ final grades than the students who lied.

**2** Listen again to check your answers. Then take turns reading a sentence each to summarize the main ideas.

**B** **GROUP WORK.** Talk about the summary.

1. What information do you find most interesting?

2. Does any of the information surprise you?

3. What do you think of the idea of lying as a social skill?

EXAMPLE    *I find it interesting that . . .*
*I'm surprised that . . .*

# SPEAKING FOCUS   *Talking about lying*

**A**   **1** SOLVE HIS PROBLEM!

**GROUP WORK.** Brian Thomas is hurrying home from work to watch the ballgame on TV. He runs a red light and a police officer stops him. Brian doesn't want to pay the $250 fine. Discuss Brian's options and write on the lines how you think the police officer would respond in each case.

| **Brian's Options** | **Possible Police Response** |
|---|---|
| 1. Say he thought the light was yellow. | _____ |
| 2. Apologize and say why he was hurrying. | _____ |
| 3. Say he couldn't see the red light because the sun was so bright. | _____ |
| 4. Other _____ | _____ |

**2** Share your ideas with the class. Decide with the class which is the best option and why.

EXAMPLE   *If Brian says he thought the light was yellow, the police officer would probably . . .*

**B**   SOCIO-DRAMA

**PAIR WORK.** Decide what to say in these situations. Choose your part and prepare your conversations. The first lines have been done for you. Role-play the conversations for the class. Does the class think you said the right things?

1. Your friend has just had his or her first baby. When you see the baby, you find it is the ugliest baby you've ever seen.

   **Friend**   Isn't she a beautiful baby?

2. Your girlfriend or boyfriend prepares a special birthday dinner for you. The food tastes terrible. You can hardly eat it.

   **Friend**   I hope you're enjoying your dinner, honey.

3. Your uncle gives you a camera as a gift. You already have two much better cameras. Besides, you don't like this kind of camera.

   **Uncle**   You will love this camera!

**C**   **GROUP WORK.** Advise these people. Share your advice with the class.

EXAMPLE   *I think John . . .   It would be a bad idea to . . .*

**John**   John has cheated on his girlfriend and feels guilty. Should he tell her or not? Why?

**Susan**   A big store has charged Susan $5 instead of $55. What should she do, and why?

**Margaret**   Margaret finds a diamond ring on the subway. Should she take it to the Lost and Found Office or keep it? Why?

## Cross-Cultural Connection

### GROUP WORK

1. Look at the following attitudes about lying. Check (✓) the ones that are true in your country, culture, or family. Talk about the attitudes and give some examples of them.

   EXAMPLE   *Lying is . . . in my culture. People . . .*

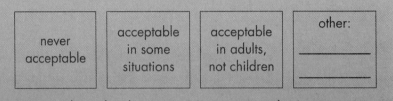

| never acceptable | acceptable in some situations | acceptable in adults, not children | other: _____ _____ |

2. Surveys show that between 30 percent and 60 percent of high school and college students in the United States cheat. Is it the same in other countries? What makes students cheat? Talk about the reasons.

# FOLLOW UP

**A** Prepare a three-minute talk to give to your group about a case that you know of, or have heard about, where people lied about something. Say if the lies were bad and if they hurt other people. Give your talk with the right stress and rhythm so your classmates understand you easily.

**B** Look at the questions in the chart below. Find out how your friends outside class feel about lying. Report their opinions to your group or class.

   EXAMPLE   *My first friend said that . . .*

| Questions | First Friend | Second Friend |
| --- | --- | --- |
| Do you think we should always tell the truth? | | |
| Are there any situations when it's better to lie? | | |
| If so, give an example. | | |

**C** Rent the video of the movie *Liar, Liar* and watch it with a group of classmates. Talk about the movie. Then discuss it with the class. Include the following:

- the character you liked best
- who the liar was
- if he *really* lied
- what Max's birthday wish was
- what happened to Fletcher in court
- the part of the movie you liked best

# 13 Environmentalist of the Year

## INTRODUCTION

1. _____    2. _____    3. _____

**A** What environmental problems do the pictures show? Match the problems in the list with the pictures. Write the problems on the lines. Then describe the pictures. Use an *Express!* question to find the meanings of new words.

> EXAMPLE   *The first picture shows . . .   There is . . .*

> air pollution        endangered animals        water pollution

**B** **GROUP WORK.** Talk about these questions. Use an *Express!* question when you don't know the word for something but can describe it.

> EXAMPLE   *One thing that causes water pollution is . . .   Another thing is . . .*

1. What can cause water and air pollution?
2. Why are whales endangered animals?
3. Do you know of any other endangered animals?
4. How do you feel when you see, or hear about, these problems?
5. What can people do to help solve these environmental problems?

**C** Read the list below of ways to help save the environment. Write one more item on the line. Check (✓) the items that you or your family do. Then tell your classmates about them, and say which items you think are important.

> EXAMPLE   *I think it's very important to . . .   I always . . . and . . .*

___ Recycle newspapers, bottles, and cans.

___ Take short showers to save water.

___ Use cloth napkins (not paper napkins).

___ Turn down or turn off the air conditioner.

___ _____

___ Use public transportation.

___ Use low-energy light bulbs.

___ Tune up your car regularly.

___ Carpool to work (share a car with other people).

# LANGUAGE FOCUS   *Topic-related vocabulary*

**A**  **PAIR WORK.** Talk about these words and their meanings. Use an *Express!* question if you don't know how to pronounce a word. Complete the sentences below. Then take turns reading the sentences to check your answers with the class.

> ≡ *Express!*
>
> Practice these *Express!* questions. If you want to help your teacher, you can say:
>
> *I'll erase the board for you.*
>
> *Can I help you hand out the PAPERS?*
>
> *I'll carry THE BOOKS for you.*

| | |
|---|---|
| **recycling** | saving things and using them again |
| **reservoir** | a pond or lake that stores drinking water |
| **toxic** | poisonous |
| **barrels** | large containers made of metal or wood |
| **dump** | to throw away trash or toxic waste on land or water |
| **marine biologist** | a scientist who studies the ocean and sea life |
| **ecosystem** | plants and animals together with their environment |
| **oil spill** | when oil comes out of a ship after an accident |
| **cleanup** | clean the sea, beaches, birds after an oil spill |
| **tanker** | a ship that carries oil |

1. My brother works at the Oceanographic Institute. He is a _____.

2. My brother studies how plants and animals live in their natural environment. He studies their _____.

3. We return used plastic bottles to the supermarket for _____.

4. The water that we drink comes from a _____.

5. The oil _____ hit another ship when it was crossing the ocean.

6. Some chemical companies _____ toxic waste into rivers and pollute them.

7. When _____ waste is dumped into rivers, many fish die.

8. Many birds and fish died after the _____ _____.

9. When tankers carry oil from one country to another, the oil is carried in containers called _____.

10. The _____ after the oil spill took many weeks.

**B**  The words below appear in this unit. Write the letter of each meaning next to the correct word. Then check your answers with the class.

EXAMPLE   *"Leak" means . . .*

___ 1. leak          a. the largest sea mammal that breathes air

___ 2. volunteer     b. a prize or honor for excellent work

___ 3. endangered    c. a piece of land with no buildings on it

___ 4. whale         d. to pass through an opening or hole

___ 5. empty lot     e. to offer to do something without pay

___ 6. award         f. when only a few animals, birds, or plants of a particular kind are left

# PRONUNCIATION FOCUS  *Intonation*

Intonation is the rise and fall of the voice. It is the tune in sentences and is closely related to sentence stress. (See Unit 6.) We use intonation to show meaning and feelings. These are some common intonation patterns.

**Falling intonation at end of sentences**

1. *Wh-* (and how) questions

Which is the most polluted city?

How much pollution is there in your country?

2. Statements

I don't know the answer to that question.

There are many endangered animals.

3. Tag questions showing certainty or agreement

It's a shame, isn't it?

We all have to help, don't we?

**Rising intonation at end of sentences**

1. Yes/no questions (can, is, do, have)

Can we help to save endangered animals?

Is there a shortage of water here?

Do you recycle newspapers?

2. Tag questions showing uncertainty

You turned off the tap, didn't you?

You are taking shorter showers, aren't you?

**A** FIRST LISTENING

- Listen to the intonation in the above sentences.
- Listen again and repeat the sentences.

**B** SECOND LISTENING: **PAIR WORK**

- Read the conversation and draw the intonation lines.
- Talk about your answers with the class.
- Listen to check them. Role-play the conversation.

Sam: This new oil disaster is terrible, isn't it?

Sue: What oil disaster?

Sam: The one in the Gulf of Mexico.

Sue: Did a tanker hit something?

Sam: Yeah. It hit another tanker and split in half.

Sue: Is much of the coast affected?

Sam: Oh, about four hundred miles.

Sue: No lives were lost, were they?

Sam: No, but thousands of birds are covered with oil.

Sue: But they can clean them, can't they?

Sam: It's not that easy. Many of them die anyway.

**A** Read the sentences below before you listen to an interview with the "Person of the Week" on a radio talk show. Talk about any vocabulary that you aren't sure of. Then listen and circle "Yes" or "No" to show which sentences have the correct information.

| | | |
|---|---|---|
| Is the "Person of the Week" Ron Dolan? | Yes | No |
| Does the "Person of the Week" live and work on the coast of Washington? | Yes | No |
| Part of his work is to rescue dolphins, whales, fish, and sea birds when they get into trouble with pollution, isn't it? | Yes | No |
| He has been a marine biologist for thirty-five years, hasn't he? | Yes | No |
| He spends a lot of his time with sea animals trying to learn what things they need in the environment. | Yes | No |
| A short time ago, there was an oil spill off the coast of Washington. | Yes | No |
| The dolphins, whales, small fish, and birds all suffered in the oil spill. | Yes | No |
| The birds had oil on their wings and couldn't fly, and they couldn't eat the fish because the fish were covered with oil. | Yes | No |
| But the fish could swim, couldn't they? | Yes | No |
| They were able to save most of the birds, weren't they? | Yes | No |
| Kevin became a marine biologist because he was fascinated with the fantastic world of the ocean. | Yes | No |
| The ocean is now full of dead fish, isn't it? | Yes | No |

**B** Listen again to check your answers. Then take turns asking and answering questions or making statements to find the main ideas with the class.

EXAMPLE    First student: *Is the "Person of the Week" Ron Dolan?*
Second student: *No, it isn't. It's . . .*
Third student: *Does he live and work on the coast of Washington?*

# SPEAKING FOCUS    *Talking about the environment*

**A** **GROUP WORK.** Every year, the state of Florida gives an "Environmentalist of the Year Award" to a person or group that helped save the environment. Which of these groups should have the award this year? Discuss the work each group did and be ready to explain your choice. Ask other groups about their choices and the reasons for them.

EXAMPLE    *All three groups are excellent, but I think that . . .*
*Which group do you think should have the award?*

### The City Recycling Group

Some teenagers discovered that very few people in their city recycled bottles, newspapers, and cans. They decided to organize a City Recycling Group. They talked to hundreds of people about why it's important to recycle and showed them how to do it. They got the city to buy five recycling trucks. They also opened a recycling center at the town dump. Now everyone in their city recycles and thousands of dollars are saved.

### The Good Gang

A group of young kids saw a TV show about how plastic trash on beaches and in the ocean kills a million sea birds and fish each year. They organized a group of volunteers to collect bottles, plastic bags, and plastic containers from the beaches near their town. Every month, the Good Gang volunteers to clean up thousands of pounds of trash in their town.

### The Toxic Team

The Toxic Team began when Jenny Jones and her neighbor discovered that a chemical company had been dumping barrels of toxic waste in an empty lot in their town. Some of the toxic waste had leaked out of the barrels and into the reservoir, where the town gets its drinking water. After months of complaining, Jenny and her group finally forced the chemical company to get rid of its toxic waste in the proper way.

**B** **GROUP WORK.** Think of two questions about some environmental problems you would like to ask the governor of your state. Write them on the lines below. Ask your group what they think of the questions.

EXAMPLE    *One of the things I would ask would be . . .    Do you think it's a good question?*

_____

_____

## *Cross-Cultural Connection*

**GROUP WORK.** Choose a country—your native country or another country that you are familiar with. Then ask one another about the country's environmental problems. Here are some examples of questions to ask. Add more questions of your own.

1. Do you have any environmental problems in your country?
2. Which is the most serious?
3. Are the people doing anything about the environmental problems?
4. Does the government have laws to protect endangered animals?

# FOLLOW UP

**A** **Make Lists!** Think of as many things to do as you can to save water in your home. Think of as many ways as you can to save electricity in your home. Bring your suggestions to class and talk about them.

### Ways to Save Water

A household can save up to 22,000 gallons of water each year. How?

> EXAMPLE *We can take shorter showers.*

1. _____
2. _____
3. _____
4. _____

### Ways to Save Electricity

We can save a great deal of electricity every day. How?

> EXAMPLE *We can use low-energy light bulbs.*

1. _____
2. _____
3. _____
4. _____

**B** **Survey.** Write a questionnaire. Make up three more questions about the environment. Ask these questions to two people in your school or community. Bring your responses to class and share them with your classmates.

| Questions | First Person | Second Person |
|---|---|---|
| 1. Would you consider buying an electric car? | | |
| 2. What is one thing you are doing in your home to help save the environment? | | |
| 3. Do you . . . | | |
| 4. | | |
| 5. | | |

**C** Prepare a two-minute talk about one of these environmental problems to give to your group or class. You can begin like this . . .

> EXAMPLE *My talk is about . . .   This is a big problem in many . . .*

air pollution     water pollution     endangered animals

# 14 Starting Your Own Business

## INTRODUCTION

**A** Talk with the class about the people and the businesses in these pictures.

EXAMPLE  *Frank Brown is the owner of a . . .*

1. What kinds of businesses do these people own?

2. How many hours a day do each of these people probably work?

3. Do you think any of these people needed a university degree to start their business? Explain.

4. Which person needed the most money to start the business and which needed the least money?

5. Which of these businesses is the most difficult to manage? Explain.

6. Would you like to own one of these businesses? Why or why not?

**B** **PAIR WORK.** Some people who open their own businesses are successful and some are not. To be successful, which of the items below do you think are important when starting a business? Share your ideas with the class.

EXAMPLE  *I think that it's important to . . .   It's not as important to . . .*

- find out how much money you need to start the business
- find out who the competition is
- know what price people will pay for your product or service
- print business cards to give to people
- have lots of experience in the field
- find a good location if you're opening a store
- buy some new clothes to make a good impression

**A** **PAIR WORK.** Can you guess the meaning of the italicized words in these sentences? Talk about what the words mean. Check your answers with the class.

EXAMPLE    *I think that "bright" means* intelligent.

1. Bonnie got a full scholarship to Harvard because she is very *bright*.

2. Toys and software that teach us something are *educational*.

3. Bob needed to know more about buying software, so he asked some *experts*.

4. Ben and Pam will need office space at home, so they will *convert* their garage into an office.

5. Phil needed money to open a business, so he *borrowed* $4,000 from his father.

6. The store has 18 different software programs to teach math. That's a good *variety*.

7. The *value* of that house is $200,000.

8. Her business *nets* $2 million a year.

> ### Express!
>
> Practice these *Express!* statements. When you arrive late to class, you can apologize and explain:
>
> *Sorry I'm late.*
> I OVERSLEPT.
>
> I FORGOT TO SET THE ALARM.
>
> THE TRAFFIC WAS BAD.
>
> I MISSED THE BUS.

**B** **PAIR WORK.** Talk about these words and their meanings. Then write the correct words in the spaces below. Take turns reading the sentences to check your answers with the class.

| | |
|---|---|
| **inn** | a small hotel |
| **marketing** | selling and advertising products |
| **software** | programs for the computer |
| **runs (a business)** | manages a business |
| **franchise** | a branch of a business chain operated by one person or a group of people |
| **online** | on the Internet |

1. McDonald's and Kentucky Fried Chicken are examples of a

   _____.

2. Vicki has computer _____ programs for many games.

3. People who can sell products on the Internet have an

   _____ business.

4. Barbara works for an advertising agency. Her major in college was

   _____.

5. When we visited Vermont, we stayed at an _____.

6. Bert has two businesses. His wife _____ one of the

   businesses.

# PRONUNCIATION FOCUS    /f/  /v/  /p/  /b/  *in initial position*

When you make the **f** sound as in *five*, and the **v** sound as in *vote*, your top teeth touch the inside part of your lower lip. The **f** sound is stronger than the **v** sound.

To make the **p** sound as in *pay*, you close your lips and blow a quick puff of air.

To make the **b** sound as in *boat*, you close your lips and blow from the back of your mouth. Put your hand on your throat to feel the vibration.

### A    FIRST LISTENING

- Listen to the **f, v, p,** and **b** sounds at the beginning of these words.
- Listen again and repeat.

| | | | | |
|---|---|---|---|---|
| fee | famous | phone | family | finance |
| van | video | variety | value | view |
| parent | pay | popular | program | product |
| begin | best | borrow | billion | business |

### B    SECOND LISTENING

- Read the pairs of words and check any new vocabulary.
- Listen carefully to the sentences and circle the word you hear.
- Check your answers with the class.

| | | |
|---|---|---|
| 1. fee   bee | 4. bet   pet | 7. Bill   Phil |
| 2. pay   bay | 5. vest   best | 8. vent   bent |
| 3. fan   van | 6. phone   bone | 9. few   view |

### C    THIRD LISTENING: **GROUP WORK**

- Read these tongue twisters aloud by yourself.
- Listen and repeat the tongue twisters.
- Practice reading them to your group.

1. Fred's famous fried fish is fantastic!
2. Vanessa sells various videos in Vernon, Vermont.
3. Barbara borrowed big bucks from the Bank of Boston.
4. Penny's play-school program is pretty popular.
5. Phil's parents bought the best possible variety of business products.
6. Val plans to borrow $50 billion to finance her video business.

**A**   Before you listen to the short talk on Virginia Vogel, read the sentences below and talk about any vocabulary you are not sure of. Use an *Express!* question if you can't hear the tape very well. Listen first for a gist of the talk. Listen again and check (✓) the sentences you hear. Then take turns with the class and read the main ideas.

___ Virginia sells a variety of software programs that teach children science, math, vocabulary, and creative writing.

___ Before her daughters were born, Virginia worked for a software marketing company.

___ Her friends asked her questions about science and math.

___ Many parents wanted to buy good software programs.

___ She could help these parents and perhaps make some money at the same time.

___ She began her business with $8,000.

___ She first sold the software in a store near her home.

___ Virginia decided that parents feel better about buying in the comfort of their own homes.

___ Virginia's parents had plenty of questions about the programs.

___ Virginia's business is called Great Ideas.

___ She now runs a business that nets $2 million a year.

 **B**   **PAIR WORK.** Read the questions below. Then listen again and talk about them. Share your answers with the class.

EXAMPLE   *Virginia's friends asked her questions ... because ...*

1. Why did Virginia's friends ask her questions about software programs for their children?

2. Who did Virginia ask to help her start the business?

3. How old are the children who would use Virginia's software programs?

4. What was one of the most important ideas that Virginia had for selling her products?

**A** **GROUP WORK.** To be successful, it is important when starting a business to think about (1) how much money you need, (2) the competition, (3) what experience you have, and (4) what the market is. Read about these people who want to start their own businesses. Talk about their backgrounds and give reasons why these people can or cannot be successful. Then talk about your opinions with the class.

> EXAMPLE    *Patty Benson . . . be successful in her business because . . .*

---

**Dog Day Care**    Patty Benson is fifty-two and is a retired teacher. Her house has a big basement and a big yard. She plans to open a dog day care business in her home. Many people who have dogs take frequent vacations and business trips. Also, there are dogs that get lonely all day when their owners are at work. She plans to charge each owner $30 a day and has $2,000 to start the business.

**A Bed-and-Breakfast Inn**    Bob and Valerie Peters, both thirty-eight, are tired of working at stressful TV jobs in the city and want to open a bed-and-breakfast inn in Bedford, Vermont. They plan to buy a six-bedroom house for $300,000 and convert it into a B & B inn. They plan to sell their condominium. The value of the condominium is $350,000. There are five small hotels in Bedford, but they feel their friendly service and bargain prices will bring them a lot of customers.

**An Online Business**    Paula and Ben Boyd own a large bookstore and want to start an online bookstore. They can buy cheap software and create their own Web page; however, they have to pay $500 a month to the Internet service company for fees and licenses. There are hundreds of bookstore businesses on the Internet.

---

**B** **GROUP WORK.** Think of four small businesses that might be successful in the future and write them on the lines below. They can offer a product or a service. Talk about them. Then explain to the class why you think they could be successful.

> EXAMPLE    *We think a . . . business could be successful . . . because . . .*

_____    _____

_____    _____

*Cross-Cultural Connection*

Choose a country you are familiar with and talk to your group about the following.

> EXAMPLE    *Small businesses that are popular in . . . are . . .*

- what small businesses are popular there
- whether people run American franchises, like Burger King
- how people usually finance their small businesses.

___ go to a bank for a loan?    ___ borrow from family?

___ plan and save ahead?    ___ other?

**A**  **1** Work with two classmates outside of class to plan a business you would like to open.

   1. First, choose the type of small business you would like to open.

   2. Then refer to section B of "Introduction" and talk about the important things you need to consider when you open a new business.

   3. Explain how you are going to advertise your product or service, the people you need to work with you, and other important details.

**2** Explain your business idea to your class. Your classmates can ask you questions about your business.

**B**  Choose two local stores that sell similar products, such as computers or other types of electronic equipment. Compare the prices in these stores and also the quality of the products. Make notes on these two stores on the lines below and tell the class about your findings.

**First Store**                                    **Second Store**

_____        _____

_____        _____

_____        _____

_____        _____

_____        _____

**C**  LOGIC PUZZLE

Five people each have a small business in the same block, next to one another. Read the statements about the people and figure out which person owns which business. Write the name of each person under the name of the business.

**Coffee Shop**   **Bookstore**   **Video Store**   **Flower Shop**   **Pet Store**

_____   _____   _____   _____   _____

1. Mrs. Fee is not the bookstore owner.

2. Mr. Berger is not the pet store owner.

3. Miss Davis is not the video store owner.

4. Mrs. Peterson's shop is next to the coffee shop.

5. Mr. Vello's shop is between the video store and the pet store.

6. Miss Davis's store is next to the flower shop.

7. Mrs. Fee's brother is the coffee shop owner.

# 15 Give Your Opinion

DO YOU THINK IT IS GOOD TO EAT ONLY VEGETARIAN MEALS?

NO, IT'S NOT GOOD FOR YOU. YOU DO NOT GET A BALANCED DIET.

YES, I THINK THAT VEGETARIAN MEALS ARE GOOD FOR YOUR HEALTH.

YES, I THINK IT IS GOOD BECAUSE IT IS WRONG TO KILL ANIMALS FOR FOOD.

**A** **1** Talk with your classmates about the picture and what is happening. Use *Express!* questions to find the meanings of new words or how to pronounce new words.

1. Which person is the moderator?

2. Who are the panelists?

3. What does the moderator do?

4. What is the name of this kind of discussion?

5. What is the question that the moderator is asking?

**2** Read the opinions of the panelists. Tell the class whose opinions you agree or disagree with and explain why.

EXAMPLE    *I agree with . . . because . . .*
*I completely disagree with . . . because . . .*

**B** **PAIR WORK.** Here are some other questions. Give your opinion about these questions. Then share your answers with the class.

EXAMPLE    *I think that families in the United States will . . .*

1. Do you think that in the future families in the United States will only be allowed to have two children? Why or why not?

2. Do you think it's better to buy a new car or a used car? Give reasons.

3. What is a good age for men to get married? And for women? Explain why.

# LANGUAGE FOCUS    *Opinion-related expressions*

**A** You will be using these expressions in this unit. Write the letter of the expressions that mean the same thing on the lines next to the numbers. Then check your answers with the class.

EXAMPLE    *"I agree with you" is another way to say...*

___ 1. I agree with you.          a. I disagree.

___ 2. In my opinion...           b. I think it's stupid to...

___ 3. I don't agree.             c. I think/I believe...

___ 4. Yes, it's true, but...      d. I think you're right.

___ 5. I think it's silly to...    e. That's right, but...

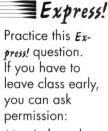

**Express!**

Practice this *Express!* question. If you have to leave class early, you can ask permission:

*May I please leave class early today? I HAVE TO GO TO THE DOCTOR.*

*I HAVE TO MEET MY SISTER AT THE AIRPORT.*

**B** **PAIR WORK.** Choose four of the above expressions to complete the conversation. Choose your part and practice the conversation.

Bob:  I think that science is more interesting than math.

Sue:  _____. I think that math is more interesting.

Bob:  What do you think about smoking?

Sue:  _____ smoke. Smoking can cause cancer.

Sue:  What do you think about diet and exercise?

Bob:  _____ exercise is more important than diet.

Sue:  _____, we also need to pay attention to what we eat.

**C** The words and expressions below are used in this unit. Write the letter of each meaning next to the number. Then make up sentences with each word or phrase and share them with the class.

___ 1. moderator     a. a group of people gathered to discuss one or more subjects

___ 2. panel         b. to exercise a lot to get rid of fat

___ 3. burn it off    c. a person who directs a discussion

# PRONUNCIATION FOCUS      /t/ talk    /θ/ think    /s/ sink

To make the sound of **t** as in *talk,* tap your tongue above your top teeth and blow a quick puff of air. When you blow, your tongue automatically drops.

To make the sound of **th** as in *think,* put the tip of your tongue between your teeth and blow.

To make the sound of **s** as in *sink,* place the tip of your tongue above the top teeth (but not touching), and then blow.

## A  FIRST LISTENING

- Listen to the **t, th,** and **s** sounds in these words.
- Listen again and repeat.

| | | | | |
|---|---|---|---|---|
| tourist | matter | boat | true | taught |
| think | health | booth | thought | something |
| sank | sin | muscle | silly | pass |

## B  SECOND LISTENING: **A Bingo Game!**

- First, read all of the words in the boxes below. There are five words across the top, five words down, and five on the diagonal. The BINGO box is "free."
- When you hear a word, look for it in the game and check (✓) it. Listen carefully.
- When a row is completely marked across, down, or diagonally, shout, "Bingo!"

| B | I | N | G | O |
|---|---|---|---|---|
| true | thank | boat | sank | pass |
| mat | thin | math | sick | tense |
| thing | boot | BINGO | both | thought |
| sin | tenth | taught | path | sing |
| three | booth | through | thick | tree |

## C  THIRD LISTENING: **PAIR WORK**

- Read the conversation aloud by yourself. Choose your part and listen.
- Listen again and repeat your lines.
- Role-play the conversation.

Edith:  Do you think thirty-three is a good age to get married?

Judith:  No, I think it's too old. Thirty sounds a better age for both men and women.

Edith:  So you are going to wait until you're thirty to get married?

Judith:  As a matter of fact, I'm getting married next month, on September tenth!

Edith:  But you're only twenty-six!

Judith:  Yes, that's true. But Sam is thirty, and I still think thirty is the best age.

**A** **1** You will hear a panel discussion with three people giving their opinions on diet and exercise. First, read the information below in each person's opinion and guess what some of the missing words are. Then listen and complete as many sentences as you can.

### Thelma Tucker

She thinks that _____ is more important than exercise.

She says that we should always try to eat _____ that are good for us.

She thinks we have to be careful to eat less _____ , less salt, and less _____ .

### Thomas Sorensen

He thinks that _____ is more important than diet.

He says that if we exercise regularly, we don't need to worry about how much fat we eat because we _____ the fat.

He says it's exercise that keeps your _____ muscles and other muscles in good condition.

### Ethan Smith

He thinks that _____ exercise and diet are important for good _____.

He says we need to _____ what we eat and exercise at least four _____ a week.

He thinks schools should _____ children about the _____ foods to eat.

**2** Listen again. Then take turns reading each person's opinions to check your answers with the class.

**B** **PAIR WORK.** Talk about the panelists' opinions. Which opinions do you agree with? Explain why. Which opinions do you completely disagree with?

# SPEAKING FOCUS    *Expressing opinions*

**A**  **1** PANEL GAME

**GROUP WORK (EIGHT PEOPLE).** Panels usually discuss one topic. You will give opinions on several topics. Choose a moderator, three panelists, and four members of the audience. The four people in the audience choose one question each to ask the panelists. The moderator should direct the discussion.

> EXAMPLE  Moderator: *Who has the first question for the panel?*
> Person in audience: *I do. My question is this: Do you think everyone should go to college?*
> Moderator: *Thank you, . . .   Would you like to start on that question, . . . ?*
> Panelist: *Well, I think . . .*

### Questions for the First Panel

- Do you think everyone should go to college?
- It's a fact that 33 percent of Americans telephone their pets and leave messages for them on the answering machine. Do you think this is a silly idea?
- In this age of advanced technology, do you think it's silly for a person to study a craft, such as weaving or woodworking?
- Do you think people should tell the truth when they know the truth will hurt the person?

**2** Now change roles. The panelists become the audience, the audience will be the panelists. Choose a new moderator.

### Questions for the Second Panel

- Do you think it's better for a nervous, impatient, disorganized person to marry someone with the same characteristics or opposite characteristics?
- Some people say it's healthier to live in a tropical climate than one with four seasons. Do you think this is true?
- Some people think it's best to spend the weekend resting and sleeping, than going out to exercise. Do you agree or disagree?
- Many people think English is easy to learn as a second language. Do you agree?

**B**  **GROUP WORK.** Do you have strong feelings about any subjects? Choose two subjects from the list, or write two others on the lines, that you have strong feelings about. Share your opinions with the group. Does the group agree with you?

> EXAMPLE  *I have very strong feelings about . . . I don't think . . .*

| | | |
|---|---|---|
| smoke-free buildings | divorce | personal ads |
| space exploration | gun-control | child adoption |
| violent TV programs | _____ | _____ |

## *Cross-Cultural Connection*

### GROUP WORK

1. Are panel discussions popular in your culture or native country? If so, explain where they hold the panel discussions (on TV, at colleges, community centers, etc.), and the kinds of questions they discuss.

2. Choose a popular topic in your culture or country. Think of two questions about the topic that you would like to ask a panel. Write them on the lines below. Talk about the questions with your group and explain why you'd want to ask them.

_____

_____

# FOLLOW UP

**A** Work with two other students outside of class to make up a story. Include the words below from this unit. The title of your story is "It's All Right for Women to Lie about Their Age." Tell your story to the class. Here is a possible beginning for your story: *This is a story about Sally. Last year, Sally . . .*

| thought | both | third | better | city |
| thirty-three | sister | silly | tonight | same |
| birthday | truth | told | something | |

**B** OPINION SURVEY

Ask three people their opinions on the following statements. The people can be students in other classes, friends, or members of your family. Write their opinions in the chart and compare them with the opinions that were given to other members of your group.

> EXAMPLE    *One person said she completely disagreed with the first statement. She thinks . . .*

1. Sometimes it's all right to cheat on tests in high school.

2. Jobs in the health or medical profession will be easy to find in the future.

3. People should eat meat or fish only once a week.

| Name of Person Interviewed | Response to First Statement | Response to Second Statement | Response to Third Statement |
|---|---|---|---|
| | | | |
| | | | |
| | | | |

**C** VOCABULARY REVIEW

Make a list of the thirty most useful words and expressions you learned in this book. Then compare your list to your classmates' lists.

# REVIEW    Units 11 - 15

## PRONUNCIATION

**A** **PAIR WORK.** Find the focus word in each sentence (the word that emphasizes an idea, new information, or a feeling or that clarifies meaning) and draw a box around it. Talk about your answers with the class. Then choose your part and role-play the conversation.

A: I have a great suggestion for you.

B: Yeah? For the field trip on Friday?

A: Yes. I suggest we rent a van and not go by bus.

B: Right. Then we can discuss the program on the way.

A: And we need to talk about the equipment to take.

B: Oh yes, I completely forgot about that!

**B** **PAIR WORK.** Read the conversation. Place dots above the words where the beat falls. Then draw the correct intonation line at the end of each sentence. (See Pronunciation Focus in Units 12 and 13.) Check your answers with the class. Choose your part and role-play the conversation.

A: Scientists say that water pollution is the biggest problem in the environment.

B: Do you believe that?

A: Well, scientists base their statements on studies, don't they?

B: I'm not so sure they do.

A: What do you think is the biggest problem?

B: Air pollution, because they're always talking about it in the news, aren't they?

A: True, but can you always believe what they say in the news?

B: Who knows. By the way, did they pass the new pollution law?

**C** **1 GROUP WORK.** Underline all of the words that start with these sounds: **f, v, b,** and **p.** Practice the words that still give you trouble.

Convenience stores, video stores, and other small family-owned community businesses have not been doing that well recently. For instance, few people drop by the corner grocery store after work to pick up something for supper now. The truth is that small businesses have trouble competing with big supermarkets and malls. These offer both a variety of products and good value, as well as thoughtful, attentive sales clerks. Customers like these things. I think it's a pity and feel very sorry that everything is changing.

**2** Now circle all the words that contain these sounds: **s, t,** and **th.** Practice the words that still give you trouble. Then take turns reading the paragraph.

# VOCABULARY

**PAIR WORK.** The four people in the following conversations are talking about their work. Complete the lines with the correct words from the lists. Take turns reading the lines to check your answers with the class. Then choose your parts and role-play the conversations.

### First Conversation

| | | | |
|---|---|---|---|
| protect | trust | relationships | suspicious |
| guilt | partners | cheat on | excuses |

Al: I understand that you help people who have problems with their

_____.

Di: Yes, I help couples deal with their feelings, such as anger and

_____.

Al: Do you find that many men _____ their partners?

Di: Yes, and then they lie to _____ their partners. But eventually the women get _____ if the men always come home late.

Al: And I suppose the women then lose _____ in their men.

Di: Yes. And they won't accept any more _____ from their

_____.

### Second Conversation

| | | | |
|---|---|---|---|
| destroyed | severe | floods | rescued |
| tornadoes | injured | damage | |

Di: You work for a disaster relief organization, don't you?

Al: Yes. We inspect disaster areas. Disasters like _____ and

_____.

Di: You mean, to see how much _____ was caused.

Al: Uh-huh. To see how _____ the damage is, if buildings have been completely _____, and so on.

Di: And I suppose you check to see how many people have been severely

_____.

Al: Right. Also if _____ people need any medical attention.

## Third Conversation

| oil spill | dump | recycling | cleanup | reservoir | get rid of |
|-----------|------|-----------|---------|-----------|-----------|

Mel:  What do you do for a living?

Kim:  I run the Environment Protection Agency, which manages

the _____ program and protects the drinking water in

the town _____ .

Mel:  Factories don't _____ toxic waste anymore, do they?

Kim:  Not often. But when they do, we force them to _____ it

in the proper way.

Mel:  Great! Have you ever had an _____ affect your part of

the coast?

Kim:  Yes. Once we had a very bad spill, and we had to do a big

_____ on sea birds and fish.

## Fourth Conversation

| loan | experts | converted | marketing | borrowed | net |
|------|---------|-----------|-----------|----------|-----|

Kim:  You're in business, aren't you?

Mel:  Yes, I _____ an old house into a candle factory last year.

Kim:  How much does your business _____ ?

Mel:  Not as much as I'd like! I _____ money to start the

business, so I have to pay off the _____ .

Kim:  Do you do your own _____ ?

Mel:  No, I get outside _____ to do that.

## EXPRESS! QUESTIONS

What can you say when you don't understand a question or an answer?

_____

_____

If you need to talk to the teacher after class or make an appointment to talk to the teacher, what can you say?

_____

_____

_____

If you want to help the teacher with different things, what can you say?

_____

_____

_____

If you ever arrive late to class, what should you say?

_____

_____

If you ever have to leave class early, what should you say?

_____

_____

# CHECK YOUR PROGRESS

**A** How much have your communication skills improved since you began this book? Write a number from 1 to 5 in each box (1 is the smallest amount of improvement, and 5 is the largest).

**Listening**     **Speaking**     **Pronunciation**

☐      ☐      ☐

**B** Identify three specific communication problems that you still have.

1. _____     2. _____     3. _____

**C** What can you do to improve your skills more? Here are some things you can do and some topics you can talk about with English speakers.

- Listen to the news in English on TV or radio. Remember some of the news items or stories that interest you. Ask your friends if they heard about them. Tell your friends about them. Ask international students about news from their countries.

- Talk to your friends about the movie *Liar, Liar*. Tell them how funny it is and recommend that they rent the movie. Ask them if they think lying is a social skill and if sometimes we have to lie to protect ourselves or other people.

- Talk to people about environmental problems and recent environmental disasters. Ask them if they think we do enough to protect the environment. Tell them what you do. Ask them what else an ordinary person can do and what governments should do.

- Ask friends who work in business how their business is doing, if their sales are good this year, if they have any new products on the market, and what they are. Find out how the business was started, how many employees there are, and if they sell on the Internet.

- Make a list of topics that interest you to talk to other people about. Give your opinion on different aspects of these topics. Ask people for their opinions; ask if they agree or disagree with you.

**D** Make notes about your plan to continue improving your communication skills.

_____

_____

_____

**E** Talk about your plans with the class and the teacher.

# TAPESCRIPTS

## UNIT 1: What Shall We Do on the Weekend?

### Pronunciation Focus, page 3

**A** Tape text as on page 3.

**B** 1. Can you cash this?
2. I want the blue chip.
3. He wants his share.
4. Yes, they are sheep.
5. She's watching the baby.
6. The museum is on Satch Street.

**C** Tape text as on page 3.

### Listening Focus, page 4

*Rich:* What are you guys doing this weekend?

*Charlie:* I'm going to watch the tennis championships on Saturday.

*Rich:* How about you, Sheila?

*Sheila:* Oh, nothing special. What do you have in mind, Rich?

*Rich:* I'd like to go fishing at Shoal Bay and maybe catch a show or movie later.

*Charlie:* There's a neat science fiction movie playing at the Odeon.

*Rich:* Yeah, I heard it has great special effects.

*Sheila:* Well, I'm not into fishing or tennis. I'll play beach volleyball with the Club.

*Rich:* OK. Why don't we each do our own thing, then catch a movie later, uh . . . around 8 o'clock?

*Charlie:* Sounds good to me! And I guess we should all read those three chapters for homework on Sunday morning.

*Sheila:* Mmm, I guess so. But maybe we can catch the pop concert Sunday afternoon at the park.

*Charlie:* Yeah! The concert is free, and the Poppin' Chicks are real cool.

*Rich:* Great! Let's check the weather forecast.

*Weatherperson:* Now the forecast for the weekend: Friday looks really good. Sunny all day with a daytime temperature of 70 degrees. But bundle up Friday night as the temperature will drop sharply. On Saturday, it will be cold and cloudy in the morning with strong winds. In the afternoon, there's a good chance of snow showers, and the temperature will only get to 37 degrees! On Sunday morning it will be cloudy, with some rain showers in the afternoon. But the temperature will rise to 50 degrees.

*Rich:* What?!

*Charlie:* Snow in *May!*

*Sheila:* They've got to be kidding!

## UNIT 2: Deals on Wheels

### Pronunciation Focus, page 9

**A** Tape text as on page 9.

**B** 1. perfect
2. expensive
3. economical
4. popular
5. beautiful
6. helpful
7. special
8. excellent
9. excited
10. classy
11. confident
12. reliable

**C**

*Mary:* Hey, Bob. Your new car is classy!

*Bob:* Yeah, it's beautiful, isn't it!

*Mary:* Yes. Was it expensive?

*Bob:* Yes, but it's economical . . . thirty-five miles per gallon!

*Mary:* And it's in excellent condition!

*Bob:* Yeah, I'm very excited about it.

*Mary:* Well, you really need a reliable car. You travel so much!

*Bob:* I know. It's the perfect car for me!

### Listening Focus, page 10

*Salesman:* May I help you?

*Woman:* Yes, I'm looking for a small car . . . something economical . . . not too expensive.

*Salesman:* Well . . . we have several good cars at the moment. The Honda over there is small and in perfect condition.

*Woman:* How much is it?

*Salesman:* Only $8,500, and it has air conditioning and new tires. It's three years old.

*Woman:* Is it an automatic?

*Salesman:* No, it's a standard shift . . . but it's very economical. It gets twenty-five miles per gallon.

*Woman:* Well, I don't like the color. What else do you have?

*Salesman:* This Ford is a fine car too. It's on special this week . . . and also in perfect condition. And it's only $6,999.

*Woman:* Oh, that's a good-looking car . . . and it's cheaper than the Honda.

*Salesman:* That's right . . . but it's not as new . . . or as comfortable, of course.

*Woman:* Does it have air conditioning?

*Salesman:* No, but it's economical. It gets thirty miles per gallon.

*Woman:* Is it an automatic?

*Salesman:* Yes, and very easy to park.

*Woman:* Well, let me look around some more. What else do you have?

*Salesman:* Well, there's the Mazda sports car on your right. That's a very classy car. And economical too. It gets twenty-eight miles per gallon.

*Woman:* Oh, it's beautiful! It's a little smaller than the other two cars.

| | | | |
|---|---|---|---|
*Salesman:* That's true. Good-looking car . . . and popular too. It's an automatic. It has air conditioning and it's newer—only two years old. It's in excellent condition.

*Woman:* Great color too. Well . . . can I take it out for a test drive?

*Salesman:* Sure, let me get the keys.

*Woman:* Oh, wait a minute . . . Is the price really $11,999?

*Salesman:* Well, yes . . . but wait till you drive it. You'll love it!

*Woman:* Forget it! Too expensive! Now, how much did you say the Ford cost?

## UNIT 3: What Are You Like?

### Pronunciation Focus, page 15

**A** Tape text as on page 15.

**B** Dale is a short, handsome man but very unfriendly. He is also impatient, especially with the children. His disorganized wife, Joyce, is no better. She's unkind to the children and sometimes is even dishonest with them. She screams at them and is insensitive to their feelings. Dale and Joyce are irresponsible parents. I think parents should be kind and compassionate with their children.

**C**

*Ted:* What's your new boss like?

*May:* Oh, he's kind of disorganized.

*Ted:* I hope he's not impatient and insensitive like the last one!

*May:* Not exactly. But he is kind of irresponsible.

*Ted:* Oh, yeah. Then he's lucky to have a responsible, organized assistant like you.

*May:* I guess so. But my colleagues say he's actually a caring, compassionate person.

### Listening Focus, page 16

*Peggy:* Hello.

*Yolanda:* Hi, Peggy. It's Yolanda.

*Peggy:* Hi. How are you doing?

*Yolanda:* Great. Listen, are you doing anything tonight?

*Peggy:* Nothing special.

*Yolanda:* Then how about coming over to meet Larry, Sam's friend from work?

*Peggy:* Sure, I'd love to.

*Yolanda:* I'll pick up some Chinese food on the way home.

*Peggy:* Sounds good. So tell me about Larry.

*Yolanda:* Uh . . . he's tall, average build, with short curly hair . . .

*Peggy:* Mmm. What's his story?

*Yolanda:* Oh. He's just getting divorced. He and his wife never got along. They are too different. June— that's his wife—is one of these sensible women and very responsible.

*Peggy:* Are you telling me that Larry isn't sensible or responsible?

*Yolanda:* Well, I'd say he's a bit impulsive, and he can be unreliable every now and again. But all in all, he's a really nice guy.

*Peggy:* Uh-huh.

*Yolanda:* June's nice, too, but she's too unromantic for Larry.

*Peggy:* Oh, yeah?

*Yolanda:* Larry's *very* romantic.

*Peggy:* Uh-huh.

*Yolanda:* I wish Sam were more romantic. But I shouldn't complain. He's really sensitive and compassionate.

*Peggy:* Sam's a great guy.

*Yolanda:* Yeah, he is. But at times he gets very nervous and impatient.

*Peggy:* Well, nobody's perfect!

*Yolanda:* That's right. See you later.

*Peggy:* Yes. Bye!

## UNIT 4: Talk about Your Country

### Pronunciation Focus, page 21

**A** Tape text as on page 21.

**B**
| | |
|---|---|
| 1. ocean | 7. season |
| 2. population | 8. industry |
| 3. desert | 9. government |
| 4. economy | 10. museum |
| 5. history | 11. talent |
| 6. culture | 12. pottery |

**C**

*George:* Maria, you're from Puerto Rico, aren't you?

*Maria:* Yes, I am.

*George:* Do you have four seasons?

*Maria:* No, we have a tropical climate.

*George:* What's the population?

*Maria:* It's over three million.

*George:* What is your main industry?

*Maria:* Tourism. It's a beautiful island.

*George:* Is your economy in good condition now?

*Maria:* Yes. There's much less unemployment than before.

### Listening Focus, page 22

*Amy:* You know, Americans like myself use a lot of Japanese products, like cars and watches, but I don't really know much about your country.

*Kenji:* Well, you know that we are a chain of islands. In the north, we have Hokkaido, where there are lots of snow-covered mountains.

*Amy:* Oh, yeah. Once the Winter Olympic Games were on Hokkaido, weren't they?

*Kenji:* Yeah. We have mountains on the other islands too. There isn't much flat land in our country. That's why the cities are so crowded.

*Amy:* I hear that Japan has a lot of earthquakes.

*Kenji:* Yes, it's true. And sometimes they're big earthquakes. The city of Kobe had a big earthquake, but most of them are small ones.

*Amy:* How often do you get them?

*Kenji:* We get earthquakes about twice a month, but we don't pay much attention to them. No big deal.

*Amy:* Oh. Well, I'd like to visit Japan next year. What places would you recommend?

*Kenji:* You have to go to Tokyo, of course, but most tourists want to go to Kyoto because it is beautiful and has so much history. And the temples and art museums are wonderful.

*Amy:* I've heard about Japanese craftspeople and would like to see some of their work.

*Kenji:* Some of the most famous crafts in Japan are pottery, woodwork, and weaving.

*Amy:* Oh, I love Japanese pottery and weaving!

*Kenji:* And what's special about the Japanese government is that it gives talented craftspeople money so they can continue working at their craft.

*Amy:* What a great idea! So the government thinks these craftspeople are very important?

*Kenji:* Yes, and the government pays special honor to craftspeople too. When only a few craftspeople are practicing a craft, the government gives it the title "intangible cultural property."

*Amy:* "Intangible cultural property" . . . Just the title sounds special!

*Kenji:* And they call the people who practice these crafts "living national treasures."

*Amy:* Well, I think it's wonderful that Japan helps its artists follow their dreams to make beautiful crafts.

## UNIT 5: Get the Message!

**Pronunciation Focus, page 28**

**A** Tape text as on page 28.

**B**

| NOT | on | watching | Donna's |
| | stopped | Doctor | office |
| **NOTE** | know | videophone | so |
| | phone | low | tone |
| **OUT** | how | couch | sound |
| | loud | outside | house |

**C** Tape text as on page 28.

**Listening Focus, page 29**

**A** *First Message*
Hello. This is the dentist's office calling. We would like to remind Bonnie that her appointment with Doctor Konlon is on Wednesday, October 30, at three o'clock. Call us at 878-0828 to confirm.

*Second Message*
Hi, honey. It's me calling at five o'clock to say that I'll be working late at the office, so don't plan on me for dinner. I'll be home around nine o'clock.

*Third Message*
Hi. This is John Jones at McBurger Restaurant calling. We found your brown pocketbook here with your wallet and credit cards. Please call us at 343-6776.

**B** *First Message*
Hello. Mrs. Johnson? This is Tony, at your house. We're about halfway through the job now, and we are just checking . . . uh . . . Are you sure you wanted the kitchen painted purple? . . . That's what you said in your note, right? Well . . . if we don't hear back from you in the next hour or so, we'll just finish up . . . uh . . . but it sure looks . . .

*Second Message*
Hi! You won't believe who just called me. Don Dole! Remember him from high school? The one with the green and yellow hair and the gold ring in his nose? Well, he's president of his own company now and making good money. We spent an hour on the phone talking about our high school days, and he sounds really nice now. He asked me . . .

## UNIT 6: Keeping Fit

**Pronunciation Focus, page 41**

**A** Tape text as on page 41.

**B**

*Daisy:* How many calories does a person need each day?

*Scott:* About eighteen hundred, I think. Why?

*Daisy:* I want to gain some weight.

*Scott:* Then you need more calories in your diet.

*Daisy:* Yes. About twenty-five hundred calories, I think.

*Scott:* Eat more carbohydrates and fats like cake and ice cream!

*Daisy:* I'm not really into sweet foods that much.

*Scott:* Well, you can eat a lot of bread and potatoes.

**Listening Focus, page 42**

*Dr. Rocco:* Well, your test results are back, Henry. Your blood tests are fine. Everything seems OK.

*Henry:* Huh. I still don't have any energy, and I get headaches all the time.

*Dr. Rocco:* Mmm. I see your weight today is 210 pounds. You've gained ten pounds since the last visit. That's a little too much for your height of five foot seven.

*Henry:* That's funny. I've just eaten the same things as always.

*Dr. Rocco:* I think maybe we should talk about diet.

*Henry:* I just eat the usual things students eat at school.

*Dr. Rocco:* The usual things . . . ?

*Henry:* Yeah, you know. In the morning, I grab a few doughnuts and a coffee on the way to school.

*Dr. Rocco:* Uu-huh. And for lunch?

*Henry:* Uh, a couple of hot dogs, fries, and a soda . . . and a chocolate bar.

*Dr. Rocco:* And dinner?

*Henry:* Pizza, chocolate pie, cookies, and soda.

*Dr. Rocco:* What about exercise?

| Henry: | Exercise? I'm not into exercise, Doctor. I just like to watch sports on TV. Anyway, I wouldn't have time for exercise . . . too much homework. |
| Dr. Rocco: | I want you to take this paper to the front desk. They'll make an appointment for you to see the dietitian. |
| Henry: | Dietitian?! |
| Dr. Rocco: | Yes. The dietitian will give you a diet to follow. I also want you to do an hour of fast walking and a one-hour workout at the gym four times a week. |
| Henry: | Diet?! Exercise?! |
| Dr. Rocco: | And then come back to see me in a month. |
| Henry: | But, Doctor, I just want some pills to give me more energy and take away my headaches! |

## UNIT 7: What Are You Afraid Of?

### Pronunciation Focus, page 49

**A** Tape text as on page 49.

**B**

| Bob: | Let's watch the ⬚sunset⬚ from the top of the tower. |
| Marge: | No, ⬚thank⬚ you. I'm ⬚petrified⬚ of heights. |
| Bob: | Oh, yeah? Then let's go on a ⬚cruise⬚ to watch the sunset. |
| Marge: | OK. ⬚Water⬚ doesn't bother me. |
| Myles: | But it bothers ⬚me⬚. I'm ⬚scared⬚ of deep water. |
| Bob: | All right. Tell me what ⬚doesn't⬚ scare you two. |
| Myles: | ⬚Flying⬚ doesn't scare us. We ⬚love⬚ flying! |
| Bob: | Then we'll watch the sunset from a ⬚helicopter⬚! |

### Listening Focus, page 50

**A** Researchers interviewed several thousand Americans to find out what they were most afraid of. Some people had two or more big fears. Although men and women feared many of the same things, more men were afraid of some things, and more women were afraid of other things. These are the results of the study.

Forty-one percent said they were petrified of speaking in front of a group in public. Thirty-two percent were terrified of heights, while many people, in fact 28 percent, were afraid of financial problems. And 23 percent were afraid of losing their jobs. Homelessness was another strong fear. Twenty percent said they were even afraid of becoming homeless one day.

Twenty-two percent were scared of deep water, and the same number, 22 percent, also feared insects and bugs. The researchers were surprised to find that only 19 percent were afraid of sickness. They were also surprised to find that just 19 percent were afraid of death. Still fewer people, 18 percent, said they were afraid of flying. Many of these people said they preferred to travel thousands of miles by car, bus, or train than take a plane. Fourteen percent feared loneliness. Fourteen percent also couldn't stand dogs and said they never went near a dog. Fewer people, only 9 percent, were frightened of driving or riding in a car. Eight percent said they were afraid of the dark. Many of these people left a light on in their bedrooms all night. And last, 8 percent said they were so terrified of elevators that they preferred to walk up twenty floors than ride in an elevator.

## UNIT 8: Watch Out!

### Pronunciation Focus, page 55

**A** Tape text as on page 55.

**B** 1. b. This is a high heel.
2. b. She often sleeps when it's raining.
3. a. The wick is almost gone.
4. a. He bit the girl.
5. a. John can fill it.
6. b. They are leaving now.

**C**

| Nelly: | Did you read about the accident this week? |
| Dean: | You mean the one on the freeway? |
| Nelly: | Yes, near Green Hill, where a pickup hit a minivan. |
| Dean: | Yeah. It seems the guy didn't see the speed limit warning on the bridge. |
| Nelly: | And it was raining so it was slippery. |
| Dean: | Uh-huh. But at least no one was killed. |

### Listening Focus, page 56

| Radio host: | You're listening to *Jazz Themes* on 93.6. Still to come is music by three new jazz artists from Memphis, Tennessee. So stay tuned, sit back, and relax! But first, we'll pause for our "Story of the Week" with Jim Green and Jean Linden. |
| Jim: | Thanks, Eric. I'll let you pick the story, Jean. |
| Jean: | OK. Well, I particularly like the one from Argentina. |
| Jim: | Oh, yeah. That's a real neat story. Let's give our listeners a quick review of it. |
| Jean: | Sure. The story took place in Buenos Aires, the capital city. Seems it started when people began hearing digging noises under a downtown street. |
| Jim: | Uh-huh. And I believe this street was near the police station. |
| Jean: | Right. At first, people joked about it, saying they must be building a new subway line under the road! |
| Jim: | Uh-huh. But the digging noises went on for weeks, so people got worried and many of them went to the police station. They warned the police that something funny was going on under the street. |
| Jean: | Yeah. And also when they saw the police on the street, they'd say, "Hey, listen. You need to investigate these noises under our feet. There's something going on under the street!" |

| | |
|---|---|
| *Jim:* | But the police didn't listen to the warnings. Imagine! |
| *Jean:* | I know! They didn't do anything. Well, yesterday, the mystery, at least, was solved when four people robbed the Credit Bank of Argentina and got away with $25 million! |
| *Jim:* | That much loot was well worth a few weeks of digging! |
| *Jean:* | Yes, indeed! |
| *Jim:* | Seems that these four guys rented a ground-floor apartment across the street from the bank and dug a tunnel under the road to the bank. |
| *Jean:* | It sounds so easy! |
| *Jim:* | Well, apparently it is, as this was the fifty-fifth tunnel robbery in Argentina in the last six years! |
| *Jean:* | Unbelievable! |
| *Jim:* | Anyone know when the next plane leaves for Argentina?! |

# UNIT 9: What Are Your Plans?

**Pronunciation Focus, page 61**

**A** Tape text as on page 61.

**B** 1. (careful)  I'm going to go to college.
2. (relaxed) I dunno what I'll do.
3. (relaxed) I wanna be a doctor.
4. (careful)  We have to go now.
5. (relaxed) Whaddya want to be?
6. (careful)  What do you want to do?
7. (relaxed) I've gotta go now.
8. (relaxed) She has alotta experience.

**C**

| | |
|---|---|
| *John:* | What are you going to do after you graduate, Mary? |
| *Mary:* | I don't know, but I have to decide soon. |
| *John:* | Yeah, I guess so. You don't have a lot of time. |
| *Mary:* | And how about you? Do you want to be a businessman like your father? |
| *John:* | No, I'm going to be a doctor. |
| *Mary:* | Uh-huh. Well, I've got to go now. Bye. |

**Listening Focus, page 62**

**A** (An example of relaxed spoken English)
*First Conversation*

| | |
|---|---|
| *John:* | Whaddya gonna do after high school, Paul? |
| *Paul:* | I'm gonna go to technical school. |
| *John:* | Technical school? You mean to learn how to be a computer technician or programmer? |
| *Paul:* | Yeah. I wanna be an airplane mechanic. |
| *John:* | How long do you hafta go to school there? |
| *Paul:* | Two years. Then I wanna get a job with an airline. And in three years Mary and I are gonna get married and buy a house. That's our dream, anyway. |
| *John:* | Sounds like a great future. |

*Second Conversation*

| | |
|---|---|
| *Anne:* | You know, Judy, you and Bob have been working for thirty years. Any plans to retire? |
| *Judy:* | Yeah. We're gonna retire in five years and move to Florida. |
| *Anne:* | Florida? That's so far away. |
| *Judy:* | Well, we're not gonna sell the house. We're gonna spend the winter in Florida and the summer in New York. |
| *Anne:* | Oh! Then everyone will wanna visit you in January or February! |
| *Judy:* | Sure! We're gonna buy a house with three bedrooms for all our visitors. |
| *Anne:* | With your big family you're gonna need a motel! |

*Third Conversation*

| | |
|---|---|
| *Louise:* | Do you still wanna be an actor, Karl? |
| *Karl:* | Yes. I'm gonna go to Hollywood and be famous! |
| *Louise:* | Oh? It's not that easy to become an actor, you know. |
| *Karl:* | Whaddya mean? |
| *Louise:* | So much competition. Every young aspiring actor goes there. And I heard alotta them hafta wait on tables to pay the rent. |
| *Karl:* | Don't worry about me! I'm gonna make it big! |
| *Louise:* | I think you're a dreamer! |
| *Karl:* | Maybe I am. But I'm gonna give it my best shot. |

# UNIT 10: In the Future

**Pronunciation Focus, page 67**

**A** Tape text as on page 67.

**B** 1. read    lead       (different)
2. cancel   cancer     (different)
3. wrong   wrong     (same)
4. lot    rot          (different)
5. right    light       (different)
6. late    late         (same)
7. arrive   alive       (different)
8. fuel    fewer      (different)
9. correct   correct     (same)

**C** Tape text as on page 67.

**Listening Focus, page 68**

| | |
|---|---|
| *Linda:* | Do you know that the world population now is five billion people? |
| *Rick:* | Five billion? Really? |
| *Linda:* | And the population is supposed to double in fifty years. |
| *Rick:* | Do you think there will be enough food for ten billion people? |
| *Linda:* | Oh, I think so. Scientists are always working to find new ways to raise crops. |
| *Rick:* | I hope so . . . and they'll probably discover new kinds of food. |
| *Linda:* | Yeah, new kinds of food . . . for ten billion people. That's a lot of food. But you know what I'm waiting for right now? |
| *Rick:* | No, what? |

| | |
|---|---|
| *Linda:* | I'm waiting for a little robot to do all my housework! |
| *Rick:* | I'd love to have a little robot! Maybe in a few years we'll be able to buy one at the mall! |
| *Linda:* | Well, I'll be right there at the store when they begin to sell them! |
| *Rick:* | Pretty soon, you won't need to go to the mall. You will be able to do all your shopping on the Internet. |
| *Linda:* | It would save me a lot of time. |
| *Rick:* | Yes, it would. Speaking of saving, what I'd like to do is try to save the environment. |
| *Linda:* | Oh, yeah? |
| *Rick:* | Yes. I'm going to buy an electric car! |
| *Linda:* | An electric car? But you can only drive a short distance and then you have to recharge the batteries. |
| *Rick:* | Yeah, it's true that you can't drive very far and have to recharge the batteries often. But electric cars don't pollute the air. |
| *Linda:* | That's true. They don't pollute. That's a good reason to use them. |
| *Rick:* | Besides, I'm not into traveling very far. |
| *Linda:* | So you're not interested in going to the moon for a vacation? |
| *Rick:* | No way. I'm a New Yorker, and I'm staying in New York. But how about you? Would you go to the moon for a vacation? |
| *Linda:* | Sure, I'd go to the moon . . . but only when there's a comfortable hotel! |
| *Rick:* | Well, let's be realistic! You won't be leaving on that trip for a long time! |

## UNIT 11: *Have You Heard the News?*

**Pronunciation Focus, page 80**

**A** Tape text as on page 80.

**B**

| | |
|---|---|
| *A:* | I heard about the tornado on the radio. |
| *B:* | Which tornado? |
| *A:* | The one in Texas . |
| *B:* | Was it as bad as the one in Louisiana? |
| *A:* | It was much worse . A hundred people were killed. |
| *B:* | That's twice as many people! |

**C**

| | |
|---|---|
| *Lisa:* | Chuck and I got married last Saturday! |
| *Bill:* | Well, congratulations ! |
| *Lisa:* | Thanks. And we've moved to another apartment. |
| *Bill:* | Boy, you have been busy! |
| *Lisa:* | Oh, and I won a medal in the ski competition. |
| *Bill:* | Wow ! |
| *Lisa:* | And I also finished my term paper. |
| *Bill:* | Great ! I haven't even started mine. |

**Listening Focus, page 81**

| | |
|---|---|
| *Erika:* | This is BCB 24-Hour News with today's top stories. |
| *Mike:* | The Tornado disaster in Florida, floods in the Midwest, and a smuggling story. All that and much more. Stay tuned! (Music.) |
| *Erika:* | The terrible tornado in Florida is first. Cindy Reed has more on the story. Cindy? |
| *Cindy:* | Erika, the damage here in Florida is just terrible! Homes were blown down the streets and completely destroyed. Cars and trucks were blown on top of the destroyed buildings. From where I'm standing, I can see a truck in a bedroom of what was an apartment building yesterday. At least forty people have lost their lives. I've just spoken to a young woman whose boyfriend pushed her into a closet, but before he could get in himself, he was blown away and killed. Cindy Reed, reporting live from Florida. |
| *Mike:* | Thank you, Cindy. Two people have also lost their lives in floods. Heavy rains caused bad floods in the Midwest. The damage is severe, and hundreds of families have been rescued from their flooded homes. |
| *Erika:* | A smuggler was caught yesterday. Thirty-two-year-old Jim Burns tried to smuggle a large python into the country . . . |
| *Mike:* | A large python?! |
| *Erika:* | That's right. He tried to smuggle a large python under his shirt. The United Nations is concerned about world poverty. The Security Council will meet to discuss world poverty tomorrow. The United Nations Secretary General wants international help to eliminate world poverty. |
| *Mike:* | Here at home, people are living better all over the country. The government said the U.S. economy is stronger than ever. And unemployment is down one percent. Now over to Mark Davies for our sports news. Mark? |
| *Mark:* | The Winter Olympics are under way, and snow conditions are great! Japan got the gold medal in ski jumping. The U.S. got the silver. At home in basketball, at the Fleet Center in Boston last night, the Lakers beat the Celtics 120 to 70. A big blow for the Celtics. |
| *Erika:* | Thanks, Mark. In our medical report, we have good news for pets. Arthritis can be hard on pets. Now, a new drug will help pets with arthritis. It takes away pain in cats and dogs. |
| *Mike:* | Coming up next on BCB 24-Hour News, another birth of octuplets. |
| *Erika:* | Wow! |
| *Mike:* | So stay tuned, and visit us online at www.bcbnews.com. |

**120** SO TO SPEAK 2

## UNIT 12: Are You Telling the Truth?

**Pronunciation Focus, page 87**

**A** Tape text as on page 87.

**B** People should always tell the truth.

This is what parents teach us.

And this is what teachers say.

Then why do we sometimes lie?

**C**

*Student:* I didn't know the exam was on Tuesday.

*Teacher:* But I wrote it on the board.

*Student:* Then I guess I completely forgot.

*Teacher:* There was no excuse for forgetting.

*Student:* I know. What can I do about it now?

*Teacher:* Nothing. You'll just have to repeat the course!

**Listening Focus, page 88**

**A** Our parents and teachers tell us that lying is bad, that we should always tell the truth. They punish us when we lie. Recently, however, psychologists have done a lot of research on lying, and they have a different view on lying.

Dr. Leonard Saxe and other psychologists say that lying is a social skill and that probably all of us lie every day. Sometimes we lie to protect ourselves. Sometimes we lie to protect other people because we don't want to hurt them by telling the truth.

Saxe did a study on lying in relationships with fifty graduate students. He was studying lying in relationships between husbands and wives and relationships between girlfriends and boyfriends. He asked the students if they ever lied to their partners. More than 85 percent said they lied, and almost all of them said they lied because they did not want to hurt their partners. For example, one student said he cheated on his girlfriend and then lied to her because he didn't want her to lose trust in him.

Saxe did another study on lying to professors. He found that sometimes students lied to professors, too. When students did not turn in a paper on time to the professor and the paper was important for their final grade, many of the students lied in their excuses. For example, a student who had a hangover because he got drunk at a party might say he couldn't turn in the paper on time because he had the flu. The professor gave students with good excuses, like being sick with the flu, more time to write the paper. But the few students who told the professor they had no excuse did not get more time to turn in the paper. Afterward, the students who said they had no excuse—in other words, the students who told the truth—were sorry they did not lie to the professor because they got lower final grades than the students who lied.

## UNIT 13: Environmentalist of the Year

**Pronunciation Focus, page 93**

**A** Tape text as on page 93.

**B**

*Sam:* This new oil disaster is terrible, isn't it?

*Sue:* What oil disaster?

*Sam:* The one in the Gulf of Mexico.

*Sue:* Did a tanker hit something?

*Sam:* Yeah. It hit another tanker and split in half.

*Sue:* Is much of the coast affected?

*Sam:* Oh, about four hundred miles.

*Sue:* No lives were lost, were they?

*Sam:* No, but thousands of birds are covered in oil.

*Sue:* But they can clean them, can't they?

*Sam:* It's not that easy. Many of them die anyway.

**Listening Focus, page 94**

**A**

*Announcer:* This is KNN Talk Radio with your host, Ron Dolan.

*Ron:* Our "Person of the Week" is Kevin Olsen. And we're glad to have Kevin here with us in the studio this evening. Kevin lives and works on the coast of Washington. His job is unusual in some ways. Part of his work is to rescue dolphins, whales, fish, and sea birds when they get into trouble with pollution. Welcome to the program, Kevin.

*Kevin:* Glad to be here. I always enjoy talking about my favorite subject!

*Ron:* You're a marine biologist, aren't you?

*Kevin:* That's right.

*Ron:* How long have you been studying marine life?

*Kevin:* Well, I've been a marine biologist for 27 years.

*Ron:* Wow! You must really like your work.

*Kevin:* I do. I spend a lot of my time with sea animals, trying to learn what things they need in the environment.

*Ron:* Uh-huh. Why are you so interested in knowing what things they need in the environment?

*Kevin:* Well, if we know what they need, we can help them survive in the future.

*Ron:* I see. A short time ago, there was an oil spill off the coast of Washington. Can you tell us something about that disaster?

*Kevin:* Yes. That was a very stressful time for us all. The dolphins, whales, small fish, and birds all suffered in that oil spill. There were a lot of problems.

*Ron:* What was the biggest problem?

*Kevin:* Well, the birds had oil on their wings, so they couldn't fly. And they couldn't eat the fish because the fish were covered with oil.

*Ron:* And I suppose the fish couldn't swim because they were covered with oil.

*Kevin:* That's right. The fish couldn't swim.

*Ron:* Sounds terrible. But you were able to save most of the birds, weren't you?

*Kevin:* No, not most of them. Only about half of them. But it took a long time and many people working on the cleanup.

*Ron:* Did you become a marine biologist because you were concerned about marine life?

*Kevin:* I became a marine biologist because I was always fascinated with the fantastic world of the ocean and how the plants and animals fit together in their ecosystem.

*Ron:* Incredible, isn't it?

*Kevin:* It sure is. But it's sad to see how human beings are polluting the ocean and destroying that ecosystem.

*Ron:* Well, let's hope there will soon be better anti-pollution laws. Thank you, Kevin, for coming in and talking to us this evening.

*Kevin:* My pleasure.

## UNIT 14: *Starting Your Own Business*

### Pronunciation Focus, page 99

**A** Tape text as on page 99.

**B** 1. John says it's a small BEE.
2. They are talking about the PAY.
3. Todd wants the large VAN.
4. It was a good PET.
5. I think this is the VEST.
6. The PHONE is on the chair.
7. Where is PHIL?
8. It was a little BENT.
9. She would like a FEW.

**C** Tape text as on page 99.

### Listening Focus, page 100

**A** Virginia Vogel is a busy young mother with a husband and two daughters ages five and three. Taking care of children is enough work for many mothers, but Virginia is also a successful businesswoman who works in an office in her own home.

What is her business? . . . Virginia sells a variety of computer software programs that teach children science, math, vocabulary, and creative writing.

How did she get interested in starting this business? Before her daughters were born, Virginia worked for a software marketing company, and when her friends with young children learned about her experience in selling software, they started asking her questions about software programs for their children. Many parents wanted to buy good software programs. The problem was that they didn't know which programs were good. They also didn't know what questions to ask about how the programs work. Virginia decided

that this would be a big opportunity for her. She could help these parents and perhaps make some money at the same time.

That was five years ago. Virginia didn't know much about children's software either, but she planned to learn more. She began her business with $8,000. She asked some experts to help her. She and the experts decided which software programs were the best for different age groups. Some programs were good for five-year-old children, and some were good for ten-year-old children.

After Virginia and the experts chose the best programs for children, she had to sell them. And how was she going to sell the software? One of the most important ideas Virginia had was to begin selling these programs in people's homes . . . not in a store.

Virginia decided that parents feel better about buying in the comfort of their own homes. She visited many homes and explained the different math, science, and vocabulary programs. This was a very popular way to present her products because parents had a lot of questions and could see more easily how the programs worked.

Virginia's business is called Bright Ideas. Virginia Vogel is a bright mother who took a bright idea and made it work. She now runs a business that nets $2 million a year.

## UNIT 15: *Give Your Opinion*

### Pronunciation Focus, page 105

**A** Tape text as on page 105.

**B** 
| | | |
|---|---|---|
| 1. sank | 7. both | 13. boot (BINGO) |
| 2. mat | 8. sin | 14. true |
| 3. pass | 9. tree | 15. sing |
| 4. thought | 10. sick | 16. booth |
| 5. tenth | 11. thing | |
| 6. through | 12. thin | |

**C** Tape text as on page 105.

### Listening Focus, page 106

**A**

*Moderator:* Good evening, ladies and gentlemen, and welcome to our program. Let me introduce this week's panel. First we have Thelma Tucker, a housewife and mother of three from South City. Second is Thomas Sorensen, a math teacher from Northtown. And third, Ethan Smith, a businessman from East Tucket. Thelma, Thomas, and Ethan, are you ready for tonight's question?

*In unison:* Yes!

*Moderator:* All right. The first question is . . . uh . . . which is more important for keeping fit, diet or exercise? Thelma, can we have your thoughts first?

**Thelma:** Sure. I think that diet is more important than exercise. Too many people eat junk food these days, and we all know junk food is not good for us. We should always try to eat foods that are good for us, like fresh fruits and vegetables. We need to avoid things like candies, cookies, and ice cream, which are bad for our health. We have to be careful to eat less sugar, less salt, and less fat to prevent serious illnesses like heart attacks and arthritis.

**Moderator:** Thank you, Thelma. What do you think, Thomas?

**Thomas:** I disagree with you, Thelma. I think that exercise is more important than diet. I mean regular exercise like workouts in the gym or running three or four times a week. If we exercise regularly, we don't need to worry about how much fat we eat because we can burn off the fat. Exercise like jogging, swimming, or even fast-walking is great. It's exercise that keeps your heart muscles and other muscles in good condition. And it also makes you feel better.

**Moderator:** Ethan, what's your opinion on this question?

**Ethan:** Well, you can't say that diet is more important or exercise is more important. Both diet and exercise are important for good health. When people believe that they can eat all the junk food they want as long as they go to the gym regularly, they are wrong. We need to watch what we eat and also exercise at least three times a week. Children should learn from an early age about the foods that are good for them. As a matter of fact, I think schools should teach children about the right foods to eat.

**Moderator:** Well, thank you Thelma, Thomas, and Ethan. And I'd like to thank you all for coming to this panel discussion. Goodnight.

# ANSWER KEY

Answers are not given for every exercise.

## UNIT 1: What Shall We Do on the Weekend?

**Follow Up, page 6**

**D** 1. children
2. chicks
3. sculptures
4. parachutes
5. church
6. sessions
7. admissions
8. century

## UNIT 3: What Are You Like?

**Follow Up, page 18**

**B**

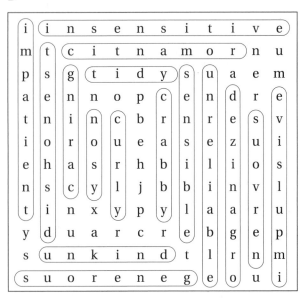

## UNIT 4: Talk about Your Country

**Language Focus, page 20**

**B** 1. b    2. a

**Follow Up, page 24**

**B** 1. Egypt
2. Australia
3. People's Republic of China
4. Cuba
5. Korea
6. India
7. Brazil
8. Saudi Arabia

## UNIT 5: Get the Message!

**Language Focus, page 26**

**B** 1. business
2. friend or family
3. family
4. friend
5. business
6. family or friend

**Follow Up, page 32**

**C** Possible answers: Joe, Ron, Don, Lonnie

## REVIEW, UNITS 1 - 5

**Pronunciation, page 33**

**A1** **Shop:** Sheila – showed – brochure – information – shore – especially – fishing – championships – should

**Chop:** Chuck – beach – watch – championships – chance – change

**Note:** *championships* contains both sounds.

**A2** **Not:** John – wants – o'clock – watch – college – want – got

**Road:** showed – brochure – know – boat – also – Joe – home – phone – only

**Down:** about – found – how – hours – around – out – now

**B** geography, climate, island, mountains, rivers, forests, industries, economy, temperature

**C** heavy, curly, handsome, unfriendly, impatient irresponsible, unreliable, disorganized, caring, compassionate, romantic

**Vocabulary, pages 34–35**

**A** b, b, a, b, a

**D** tropical, seasons, earthquakes, unemployment, economy, manufacturing, exports

**E** 1. d    2. e    3. b    4. a    5. c

## UNIT 6: Keeping Fit

**Speaking Focus, page 43**

1. **F.** According to the Surgeon General's report on exercise, walking or bicycling is just as good as jogging to keep fit.
2. **T.**
3. **F.** Muscle is made up mostly of water: 70 percent is water and 22 percent is protein.
4. **F.**
5. **T.**
6. **F.** Allow at least two hours after eating before working out.
7. **T.**
8. **T.** If you're shaped like an apple, your waist is as big as your hips, which means you probably weigh too much.
9. **F.** A balanced meal has some carbohydrate, some protein, vegetables, fruit, and very little fat or sweets.
10. **T.** They reduce stress.

## UNIT 7: What Are You Afraid Of?

**Follow Up, page 52**

**C**
1. sickness
2. petrified
3. homeless
4. terrified
5. loneliness
6. can't stand
7. sidewalk
8. frightened
9. financial
10. microphone

## UNIT 8: Watch Out!

**Language Focus, page 54**

**B** *First picture:* Hold it there! Halt!
*Second picture:* Freeze! Don't move!
*Third picture:* Hands in the air! Hands up!

## UNIT 9: What Are Your Plans?

**Follow Up, page 64**

**C**

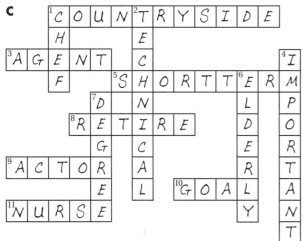

## REVIEW, UNITS 6 - 10

**Pronunciation, page 73**

**A Bit:** is – driving – stopping – speeding – leading – giving – ticket – in – him – carrying – big

**Beat:** Dean – he – sees – policeman – speeding – street – leading – freeway – thief – leaps – TV

**Note:** *speeding* and *leading* contain both vowel sounds.

**B** These are the most likely words to be stressed and highlighted:

*A:* Sara spends |hours| exercising every day.

*B:* Well, she's so |afraid| of getting sick.

*A:* Yes, but just |one| hour of exercise is enough.

*B:* True. I |never| exercise for more than one hour.

*A:* Uh-huh. But |you| are not afraid of getting sick.

*B:* No, but I'm scared of |other| things!

*A:* I'm sure |everyone| is scared of something.

**C**
*A:* What do you want to do tonight?
*B:* Study. I have to write a paper.
*A:* I'm going to watch the ball game.
*B:* I've got to go. I've a lot of stuff to do.

**Vocabulary, page 74**

**A** watch out, cool it, slow down, in good shape, put on, can't stand, not into, brought up

**B**

```
x (p r o t e i n) x  p
z (e) y (v e l c r o) e
s  m  d i o v a t p  t
e  b  g (g o a l) c o  r
k  a (s p o r c r l) i
a  r (f r e e z e) l  f
n  r (r e c n a c) u  i
s  a  j (h a l t) k  e
u  s (e r i t e r) e  d
s  s (g n i r i p s a)
```

## UNIT 11: Have You Heard the News?

**Follow Up, page 84**

**C**

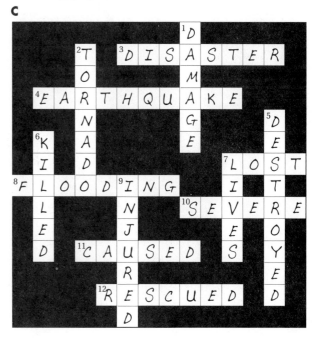

## UNIT 14: Starting Your Own Business

**Follow Up, page 102**

**C**

| | |
|---|---|
| **Coffee Shop** | Mr. Berger |
| **Bookstore** | Mrs. Peterson |
| **Video Store** | Mrs. Fee |
| **Flower Shop** | Mr. Vello |
| **Pet Store** | Miss Davis |

## UNIT 15: Give Your Opinion

**Language Focus, page 104**

**A** 1. d    2. c    3. a    4. e    5. b

## REVIEW, UNITS 11 - 15

**Pronunciation, page 110**

**A** These are the most likely words to receive focus:

| | | |
|---|---|---|
| great | field | van |
| program | equipment | forgot |

**B**

*A:* Scientists say that water pollution is the biggest problem in the environment.

*B:* Do you believe that?

*A:* Well, scientists base their statements on studies, don't they?

*B:* I'm not so sure they do.

*A:* What do you think is the biggest problem?

*B:* Air pollution, because they're always talking about it in the news, aren't they?

*A:* True, but can you always believe what they say in the news?

*B:* Who knows. By the way, did they pass the new pollution law?

**Vocabulary, pages 111–112**

*First Conversation*
relationships, guilt, cheat on, protect, suspicious, trust, excuses, partners

*Second Conversation*
floods, tornadoes, damage, severe, destroyed, injured, rescued

*Third Conversation*
recycling, reservoir, dump, get rid of, oil spill, cleanup

*Fourth Conversation*
converted, net, borrowed, loan, marketing, experts